Work THE Problem

OW EXPERTS
ACKLE
ORKPLACE
HALLENGES

STAFFORD

atd
PRESS

© 2018 ASTD DBA the Association for Talent Development (ATD)
All rights reserved. Printed in the United States of America.
21 20 19 18   1 2 3 4 5

No part of this publication may be reproduced, distributed, or transmitted in any
form or by any means, including photocopying, recording, information storage
and retrieval systems, or other electronic or mechanical methods, without the prior
written permission of the publisher, except in the case of brief quotations embodied in
critical reviews and certain other noncommercial uses permitted by copyright law. For
permission requests, please go to www.copyright.com, or contact Copyright Clearance
Center (CCC), 222 Rosewood Drive, Danvers, MA 01923 (telephone: 978.750.8400;
fax: 978.646.8600).

Author photo by Jeffrey Crespi

ATD Press is an internationally renowned source of insightful and practical
information on talent development, training, and professional development.

All names, characters, places, or incidents referenced in *Work the Problem: How
Experts Tackle Workplace Challenges* are fictional, and any resemblance to actual
persons, entities, places, events, or incidents is coincidental. Further, *Work the
Problem* summarizes the perspectives of the author and contributors only and does
not constitute the opinion, policy, approval, or endorsement of ATD.

ATD Press
1640 King Street
Alexandria, VA 22314 USA

Ordering information: Books published by ATD Press can be purchased by visiting
ATD's website at www.td.org/books or by calling 800.628.2783 or 703.683.8100.

Library of Congress Control Number: 2018938439

ISBN-10: 1-947308-57-2
ISBN-13: 978-1-947308-57-2
e-ISBN: 978-1-947308-58-9

ATD Press Editorial Staff
Director: Kristine Luecker
Manager: Melissa Jones
Community of Practice Manager, Career Development: Lisa Spinelli and Sue Kaiden
Developmental Editor: Caroline Coppel
Text Design: Iris Sanchez
Cover Design: Faceout Studio, Allison Nordin
Printed by Versa Press Inc., East Peoria, IL

To everyone stuck, panicked, or myopic,
who yearns to be strategic

CONTENTS

FOREWORD

In today's world of work, increasingly complex organizational and management structures make being an employee and a manager harder than ever. We're highly interconnected, fiercely competitive, knowledge driven, and global. The markets are chaotic, resource needs are unpredictable, and we are geared for constant change. As a result, employers must be lean and flexible to survive. Employees, in turn, are less likely to trust the system to take care of them over time, and thus less likely to make immediate sacrifices in exchange for promises of long-term rewards. They are more likely to disagree openly with their employers' missions, policies, and decisions, and challenge employment conditions and established reward systems.

Traditional sources of authority are also being steadily supplanted by new ones. Seniority, age, rank, and established practice are diminishing. Organization charts are flatter; layers of management have been removed. Reporting relationships are more temporary; more employees are being managed by short-term project leaders instead of "organization-chart" managers. More transactional forms of authority are also on the rise, such as control of resources, control of rewards, and control of work conditions. Employees look to their immediate supervisors to meet their basic needs and expectations, and freely make demands of their managers. Managers who cannot meet these needs have less and less authority in the eyes of their direct reports.

Meanwhile, most middle managers, like everybody else, have more tasks and responsibilities of their own, along with more administrative duties. In addition, managerial spans of control—the number of employees officially reporting to each supervisor—have increased, and managers are also more likely to manage remote employees. The breadth and complexity of the work being done by the employees reporting to each manager has probably also expanded.

Most people would rather work in effective organizations with outstanding managers. Organizations that consistently deliver the highest quality and service develop their employees and have clear lines of communication up, down, and across the organization. People want to work for organizations with clear missions, goals, and reporting relationships and flawless processes. Unfortunately, finding that is much harder than ever before, and it's getting harder every day.

The 10 case studies in this book offer a look into the sort of complex and interwoven challenges that people face in the workplace today. Much like a business school intensive seminar, *Work the Problem* applies the classic case study pedagogy to the challenges of workplace dynamics. Grounded in very real-world scenarios, the case study method allows the reader to contemplate 10 different sets of circumstances, each with its own issues, cast of characters, and range of perspectives. The cases deal with such a range of issues—corporate culture, organizational structure, market shifts, technology, change leadership, chain of command, authority and accountability, communication, performance management, and career paths—that they become relevant to anyone.

While they find themselves in a wide range of positions in a number of different organizations, the key players in each case study are stuck in the middle of a number of stakeholders—their manager and those they manage as well as various other constituents—trying to negotiate their competing needs and expectations. Most of us would rather avoid these types of conflicts. In the old long-term hierarchical model (the pyramid organization chart), followers took for granted their managers' authority and the authority of the employer. As a result, followers were more likely to figure out what to do, and do it, making lots of mistakes along the way, no doubt. But there was more room back then for waste and inefficiency. Not anymore.

These case studies provide so much food for thought, like a shortcut to real workplace experience. Because they are so realistic, there are no 100 percent correct answers and no easy solutions. This is evident in the two commentaries from industry experts following each case study. The nine commentators offer analysis and recommendations in response to the challenges raised in the different scenarios—they're like a professor's input on the case, helping the student understand what's really going on, while also providing a framework for how one might begin approaching such a challenge in the real world.

Work the Problem is for those of us in organizations that aren't perfect but that we need to work within to navigate and affect change from the middle, and for those who need to become better skilled so we can find and support those organizations that more closely approach our ideal.

—Bruce Tulgan
June 2018

ACKNOWLEDGMENTS

To the many creative, smart, caring, talented, deserving, ambitious, thwarted, frustrated, exhausted, reflective, funny, generous, and, most of all, hard-working people who shared their work-life stories with me—thank you for your time, patience, interest in the project, and anonymity. My hope is that you don't recognize yourselves at all in the following pages, but at the same time you feel vindicated and supported by the commentaries.

Thank you to Sue Kaiden, former ATD Career Development Community of Practice manager, who partnered in guiding this book forward and developing its commentaries. Every subject matter expert appearing here was her inspired choice, and from the start, her interest and energy gave the book project a form, structure, and purpose when my own sense of those things sometimes flagged.

I've bent the ears of numerous ATD colleagues over the last couple years, and am grateful to Jack Harlow, Melissa Jones, Caroline Coppel, Kris Luecker, and Christian Green for their editorial guidance, abiding interest, and enthusiasm. Courtney Cornelius and Hannah Sternberg offered fresh and expert eyes. Ryan Changcoco also gave helpful and insightful feedback.

I deeply appreciate Deborah Orgel Hudson, Kristen Fyfe-Mills, Avra Bossov, and Alex Moore for their efforts creating the marketing wind beneath this book's wings, or giving it wings at all.

Chris Adams, Vivian Blade, Alan De Back, Glen Earl, Tom Kaiden, Sharlyn Lauby, Ben Locwin, Rick Rittmaster, and Joe Willmore—thank you for your intelligence, expertise, generosity, creativity, and collegial spirit, all of which made this book better than what I imagined. You've taught me a lot—thank you for being part of this virtual conversation.

Jeff Crespi, daily work whisperer, thank you for insightfully working all problems.

INTRODUCTION

"Work the problem." It's a phrase I often heard growing up, and I always believed it was specific to engineering. I was an aeronautical engineer's daughter, so this made sense. I knew how my father used it—when I didn't understand how two variables worked in trigonometry and the broken pencils were gathering under the dining room table at my feet (why was I taking trig anyway? I wanted to be an English major!), my father would say, "Just work the problem!"

It was a frustrating thing to hear because it suggested that solutions were simply lying under the surface, just beyond my attention. If I could truly see them, if I could calm my mind and focus, I could . . . work the problem.

This was also the advice my brother's high school chemistry teacher would give. "The information is always there," my brother remembers him saying. "But sometimes it is hidden or not relevant. Read the problem. Read it again. Work the problem, people."

I didn't know then how people beyond the scientists of my youth used this phrase in their daily lives, or if they even did. But today, working the problem is a concept we all understand in our organizations and in our working lives. And, it has inspired this book. How do we manage difficult problems at work? When things become difficult, do we have the resources we need to work the problem? And more important, how do talent development professionals respond? What do subject matter experts say?

For example, imagine you are in this webcast audience:

> The new book author guesting on workplace innovation has just finished her presentation and is getting

ready to take questions. She is energetic and compelling, discussing how to implement the drivers of innovation into the office, work with teams to be creative and productive, encourage bosses to allow ideas to flow, and hire people who love what they do.

When the first question comes—it seems inevitable, really.

"What if everyone but your boss is on board? What do you do if your boss is the obstacle to the innovation you and others envision? My manager is the problem. What do I do?"

You hear the author emit a groan, a grunt of familiarity, even empathy, before capitulating. Without hesitation she replies: "I'd quit."

Then silence.

Grudgingly, you admit that you can understand her response. In fact, it's supported by data. Gallup has long reported that people leave jobs because of their managers. And a 2013 Accenture study showed that while many employees would like to innovate, they aren't supported from above. In addition, the majority of company leaders responding to a 2016 global survey by the O.C. Tanner Institute reported that while they had the encouragement, time, and resources to do their work or innovate, less than half of their employees said the same. Employee engagement is at record low numbers, but the engagement numbers for managers aren't much higher.

So, when thinking about how I'd respond to that caller, I began to ask myself, "What would you do?"

That question ultimately led to virtual conversations with nine subject matter experts about what they would do when faced with seemingly intractable problems beyond their control. I sent them stories I'd written—fictionalized case studies—and asked them the questions we all want the answers to: "If this were your job, and if this were your problem, what would you do? How would you work the problem? Or would you quit?" Their answers were many, varied, entertaining, and so well informed. The whole process heartened me, and I hope it does the same for you to see how many ways exist to work our problems.

Work the Problem is for anyone who has ever encountered workplace problems and sought expert advice or solutions to broaden their understanding of their own predicaments.

How It's Organized

Each fictionalized case study in this book is based on interviews I conducted with a variety of anonymous sources, supported by research and statistical data. Each case study is then followed by commentary from two subject matter experts drawn from the following—Christopher Adams, Vivian Blade, Alan De Back, Glen Earl, Tom Kaiden, Sharlyn Lauby, Ben Locwin, Rick Rittmaster, and Joe Willmore.

As you read this book, you will see that a key focus is managers in the middle. The goal was to present situations in which managers needed to navigate and influence change or manage their situation "up." This is a particularly valuable perspective because most leadership books talk about what CEOs and senior leaders should do, but don't necessarily talk about it from the perspective of people in the middle.

Here's a closer look at each chapter:

- Case Study 1: Family Fade-Out—Faced with market changes, a once-successful family-owned electric light products business is struggling, and its inexperienced though tech-savvy manager of operations meets resistance in the warehouse.
- Case Study 2: "Did You Read the Memo?"—Changes at a once-respected foundation under new leadership are creating problems for its top fundraiser.
- Case Study 3: Driving the Bus—A woman software engineer manager at a tech start-up is facing challenges.
- Case Study 4: "All My People Are Great"—A longtime tech manager in a global corporation is feeling pinched by HR.
- Case Study 5: No Room at the Top—A Millennial editor is overworked and frustrated by the lack of transparency and room for promotion at a small media company.

- Case Study 6: Spread Thin in the Middle-Management Sandwich—A marketing director in a city with tourism growth possibilities is caught between a micromanaging CEO and direct reports who are juggling excessive responsibilities.
- Case Study 7: "It Couldn't Happen Here"—A longtime successful bank branch manager is forced to make some choices when her staff is poached by a rival branch.
- Case Study 8: "We've Always Been Fine"—A third-generation family hotel is struggling in the modern hospitality world.
- Case Study 9: A New College Director Sees Only Faculty Myopia—A young director gets the job of his dreams, but finds himself rudderless and without authority.
- Case Study 10: Maneuvering the New Healthcare—A patient care representative tries to manage disruptions at her workplace while staying true to her profession's wellness ideals.

1

FAMILY FADE-OUT

Cast of Characters at Lightgate Supplies

Theo Paine—Operations Manager

Sam Winston—Warehouse Employee

E.B. Callaway—CEO

Evie Marshall—Warehouse Manager, Staff Supervisor, HR

Gabe Earnest—Warehouse Manager, Inventory, Security, Safety

"Fire all the managers," said Sam Winston as he walked into the CEO's office. That was all Theo Paine heard before CEO E.B. Callaway quickly shut the office door. The occasion was Sam's going-away party, and the CEO had a habit of collaring favored longtime employees at such events and cajoling them to answer: "If you ran the warehouse, what would you do?"

But as operations manager, Theo Paine did run the warehouse—and he had to hand it to Callaway; once people were out the door, or shown it, the CEO had a sudden flair for candor.

Lightgate Supplies had recruited Theo to be its new operations manager only a few months ago. It was a job, Theo thought, he was too young for at age 30. Nevertheless, it was a position he aspired to and could hardly refuse. As a college student, he had worked in the Lightgate warehouse during summer breaks, and was a well-regarded employee. Mixing easily with the full-time warehouse staff, he was relied on by supervisors and workers alike. Theo studied information technology in college and was intrigued by supply chain dynamics. After getting an A+ certification, he served a couple stints as a tech on organizational help desks while considering whether to pursue a manufacturing tech management program. Then he got the call about Lightgate. Theo knew the company wasn't state of the art by any means, but it was a place where he thought he could get the supply chain experience he desired, and even try to make Lightgate's glacial product distribution processes a little more high tech.

But there were problems at Lightgate of which Theo was unaware when he came on board. In the last four years, a series of operations managers had come and gone—the last one, who had been popular on the warehouse floor, had left suddenly when sales on the new product lines wouldn't budge. The CEO hadn't been able to persuade either of his top candidates to take the job, despite salary offerings he knew were competitive. Word was out that Lightgate, which once had been a small yet reliable industry star, was lagging behind its competitors and scrambling to hold position.

Lightgate Supplies

Lightgate Supplies, a U.S. company headquartered in suburban Maryland, was founded in 1884 by Cyrus Callaway, a banker, and his son, Daniel, an engineer. Over the early 20th century, the company became one of the largest lighting manufacturers and suppliers of carbon filament lamps in the region. Eventually, the Callaway family separated out the more profitable lighting manufacturing division from the supply and distribution company and sold it to a larger manufacturing enterprise. During recent decades, Lightgate focused on lighting solutions for retail, office, and the home, as well as establishing two stores to sell the lighting products in its central distribution warehouse. The company recently reported an annual revenue of $20 million and currently employs 50 people in its two stores and warehouse.

Lightgate's primary customers are contractors for the building trades who prefer face-to-face contact with their suppliers, although the percentage of online sales has been increasing steadily over the past decade. The Lightgate brand is one of the oldest in lighting supply on the East Coast, and similar companies are challenged to compete with its prestige. Its mission statement, "Using the best technologies to meet the toughest challenges, we make the future brighter," highlights the company's enduring commitment to excellence and innovation.

However, with the recent shift from incandescent bulbs to LEDs, the lighting industry has been undergoing dramatic changes akin to the first lighting revolution Thomas Edison sparked well over a century ago. The landscape for competitors is changing overnight because of this new technology. Replacement bulb sales are becoming a thing of the past, and intersystem communication is the future—not just smart bulbs, but smart systems that are interconnected and lighting-based. Because LEDs are smaller, last longer, and use less energy, they create more product options, diverse design systems, and ways to stock appliances. Lighting companies are increasingly joining up with IT to create smart solutions for a variety of uses, which also opens up more options for service contracts.

It's uncertain if a company like Lightgate, founded in the 19th century on old technology, can adapt and thrive in this new atmosphere.

Wanted: Stability in the Warehouse

As Callaway read the latest quarterly report, he sighed. It was bad, and the CEO knew there would be increasing pressure from the board to cut costs, freeze expenditures, maybe even lay off employees or close a store. How could he continue to be positive about the prospects of the company he led, yet candid about its situation?

He was searching for yet another operations manager, and no one would take the job, despite competitive offers. Then Theo Paine's resume, along with his thoughtful letter, were brought to his attention. Callaway remembered him as a people person, who had both the smarts to understand the product lines and the ability to chat up contractors and salespeople alike. He knew that Theo understood the insular warehouse culture, thanks to his time as a summer worker, and believed that he could persuade the crew to work more efficiently and effectively. That Theo was young—and unlikely to push him on salary—wasn't lost on Callaway either.

During the interview, Theo impressed Callaway with his easy, conversational knowledge of new product lines that were proving difficult to move, even suggesting sales force training and some off-sites for store personnel. Here was a young man, thought the CEO, with great business instincts.

Callaway wanted his new operations manager to "stabilize things down there" in the warehouse. He knew that employee turnover was high, morale and pay were low, and product damage was a growing problem. And he believed that young Theo Paine, whose first job was on Lightgate's warehouse floor, just might be the perfect person to fix the company's problems.

High Turnover, Low Morale

Theo had been optimistic during his first few months as Lightgate's operations manager, despite his inexperience. He fondly remembered the warehouse managers—Evie Marshall, who supervised the staff and ran HR, and Gabe Earnest, who was in charge of inventory, security, and safety—from his earlier stint at the company. Both had been at Lightgate for nearly two decades, and Theo hoped to rely on them for support and institutional knowledge while he got up to speed on the warehouse operations. And, as he kept reminding himself, Evie and Gabe, for better or worse, had been members of the adult working world much longer than he. They were pros and knew the ropes. He didn't expect any resistance. Rather, Theo intended to focus on the

20 or so full-time warehouse workers—those who did the lift driving, picking, packing, receiving, and stocking. They were the heart of the operation, and their morale and retention were key.

As Theo walked the warehouse floor, he immediately noticed that many things had changed since his first stint at Lightgate. The water-coolers had been moved from the warehouse floor to the break room. Security cameras had been installed, although they'd been placed in the main area where the trucks came in and were easy to avoid. He saw that the hoodies everyone seemed to prefer, while warm in the cold warehouse, blocked the workers' peripheral vision. He also couldn't find any ergonomic tools or aids. More alarming, no one wore safety shoes, and not only were work gloves rarely worn, they were no longer issued.

Theo learned that, in a cost-cutting measure, Gabe had "temporarily" eliminated the safety bonuses, line per hour bonuses, and damage bonuses. The incentives he had introduced in their place, many workers complained, were out of reach. What's more, the monthly safety lunches, which Theo fondly recalled, were a thing of the past—few current staff even remembered them. There also hadn't been a company-sponsored family picnic day in five years.

The warehouse workers were assigned to two overlapping shifts: the first from 6 a.m. to 2 p.m., and the second starting at 11 a.m. and ending at 7 p.m. or until the trucks were unloaded. The bulk of the damages seemed to occur in the later hours. Some mornings Theo would come in to find baskets of broken and damaged light fixtures and systems, as if someone were quietly vandalizing products overnight, then carefully collecting and counting them. The whole anonymity of it was wearing on Theo. He believed the only way to solve his problem was to work alongside the employees during those busy times, so he could watch the forklift speeds, the sharp corners taken, and the overloaded pallets. If necessary, he could retrain on the spot.

But Theo couldn't be everywhere, and damages continued to happen. He wondered if changing the shifts to create a gap in between would help. Was the overlap creating chaos from warehouse crowding? Maybe a gap between shifts would allow time for catching up, cleaning up, and maintenance. And there could be other contributing factors. For example, was the warehouse layout logical? Product bins were arranged throughout the warehouse floor, but the challenge of finding and locating items in a place the size of four football fields was greater for new workers who weren't familiar with the inventory. Bottlenecks and slowdowns were common, and products were misplaced and misfiled all the time. Theo thought that better naming conventions would help the less experienced workers. He also noticed that faster-moving products weren't always placed near the best picking lanes—could something be done about that? Perhaps if he organized each shift into smaller groups to assign them to specific areas of concern. But that would take more staff than he currently had, wouldn't it?

One of the first things Theo did as operations manager was institute a smartphone policy. It seemed obvious to him that phones on the floor led to distracted employees, broken products, and personnel injuries. In fact, he was surprised that Evie Marshall hadn't insisted workers leave their phones in their lockers and check them only when they left the floor during breaks and lunch. However, this new policy was difficult for him to enforce when the warehouse managers kept their personal phones in plain sight despite the new policy; he heard their melodic ringtones throughout the day.

New employee orientation was Evie's domain, but when Theo observed that there was no training beyond what everyone received for safe forklift operation, he created a module on safe warehouse operations. Unfortunately, the steady stream of new workers and truck deliveries backing up in the yard forced him to put the training on hold. When Theo asked Evie why she wasn't supporting his module, she explained that she always waited for new employees to pass a six-month probationary period before investing in "costly, time-consuming training." In response, Theo thought about assigning an experienced worker to take over the training or trying to pair new workers with veterans, but first he had to identify workers who could act as mentors. There weren't many veterans, as the average tenure for a warehouse worker these days was three to four months, and Evie interviewed daily.

"I'd get suspended for the way they behave."

Sam Winston was one of Lightgate's few remaining longtime employees. Theo remembered him from his college days, regaling the crew with hunting stories from his Maine boyhood or his stint in the U.S. Air Force. He'd once been a floor supervisor at one of the big box stores, but said he tired of all the forced overtime. He was a grandfather now, and weekends were for his family, he'd say; let the younger generations do the extra shifts.

All the workers, new and old, respected Sam, so Theo thought that enlisting his help in training and orientation would be the way to go. Sam knew compliance and how to be safe on the job. He also understood and cared for the product lines. But when Theo asked Sam for his help, the older man balked.

"It would have to be for a significant raise in pay," Sam said. "Do you know what the new guys—half my age—are getting? It's criminal."

"I can try to do something about that," Theo replied. "We can help each other here." He knew that Evie, eager to attract more experienced applicants, had increased the starting wage for new warehouse workers, so loyal longtimers like Sam were barely earning more than the rookies.

"You always seemed like a nice kid," Sam said, "but you're out of your league, son. Those other so-called managers—Evie and Gabe—I'd get suspended for the way they behave. They don't walk the floor, don't follow their own safety regulations, and they fire people at the drop of a hat."

Theo remembered Sam as a company leader, smart, outspoken, hardworking. But when he went to talk to Evie about Sam's position, she told him that Sam would bicker with her over floor regulations, and that once she'd had to send him home for arguing with her.

"That's crazy, Evie," Theo said. "We all lose when people get suspended like that. Sounds like high school!" Then he bit his tongue, but it was too late. Evie was careful around Theo after that.

"It feels like a jungle."

Theo started each day on the warehouse floor with the first shift. These were the more experienced workers, the core whom he expected to set the tone for the day—unpacking delivery trucks as they arrived, putting away stock, pulling store orders, wrapping and piling pallets, flying around on their forklifts, and scanning as many lines an hour as they could manage. Chaos, then silence.

The second, less experienced shift was larger, younger, and noisier. While their supervisors were on the premises until the trucks were emptied and the shifts ended, no matter how late, they never ventured into the warehouse. At first Theo stayed, too, hoping that the 12- and 14-hour days would not become custom, but they soon did.

Gabe told Theo that he shouldn't work on the warehouse floor with the shift employees; instead, he needed to "find a way to manage without mixing it up, to keep respect." Gabe also prided himself on being a safety specialist, subscribing to all the current publications on warehouse best practices. He knew OSHA regulations and distributed the agency's pocket guides on worker safety to each new employee. As they talked in Gabe's office, Theo could see the OSHA guides in an open box on the floor. On the wall behind the desk were two gilt-framed awards and a faded photograph of Gabe and the CEO shaking hands in the middle of a concrete field 20 years ago.

"I think you're wrong about the importance of training," Gabe continued. "I never received any training on the job, but I've stayed up-to-date with everything, despite the effort it took with all the personnel changes. They're very disruptive and make it hard on everyone. Sometimes, it feels like a jungle in the warehouse, and we're all just trying to keep up."

According to company records from the past year, Gabe had fired employees for product damage during their shifts, as well as failure to show up at all, which continued to be a problem. When Theo asked him about weighing the cost of retraining versus rehiring, Gabe said that while he understood Theo's "staffing problem," those fired employees had increased the risk level for everyone, and that he had to set a consistent policy to "send a message."

"Given the current climate," Gabe admitted, "there are few opportunities for advancement." But he agreed with Theo's request to institute weekly staff safety meetings and to support his experiment in creating a gap time in the two labor shifts.

* * *

In his four months on the job, Theo had seen close to 70 percent employee turnover in the warehouse, and reported product damage approaching $30,000 a month. His warehouse supervisor was holed up in her office and appeared afraid of her staff, and his safety chief was cool to training.

It was time to talk to E.B. Callaway.

"You expect a lot from a little light bulb."

Theo hadn't talked to or seen Callaway in weeks, and the CEO didn't like email. So, on a quiet afternoon before Sam's going away party, the two men walked through the warehouse, greeting the workers who were straightening up aisles as they headed toward the delivery truck bay.

"We could cut product damage in half just by offering a monthly bonus," said Theo. "And then with even informal training and safety talks, things should start to stabilize before I make some physical warehouse improvements. We'll start to turn things around by next quarter."

The CEO paused. "Improvements like what? Right now, your improvements are slowing us down."

Theo chose to ignore Callaway's statement, and simply focused on the question. "Add more smart lighting. Some areas are a safety hazard. The lighting should improve morale, too; people complain about it. And then some product tracking."

Callaway had been forthright with Theo when he hired him, describing a growing "disconnect" among employees in the warehouse.

But Theo sensed a growing impasse with his boss on the company's more intractable problems of morale and turnover.

"You expect a lot from a little light bulb, don't you, son? Sales are down this quarter, and it's because of your shift problems. You're not getting product out in a timely manner. And from what I can tell, you've slowed things down to just make them cleaner."

Suddenly the two men realized that both day shifts plus Evie and Gabe were standing within earshot of the warehouse dock and watching them.

Startled, Theo stopped, but the CEO kept walking and called over his shoulder to the younger man: "Reduce the damages first. Show me how we'll make money investing in the warehouse, and you're a genius."

TAKE 1

Commentary by Joe Willmore

A leader in the field of human performance, Joe Willmore is a consultant for a range of organizations and the author of numerous publications on performance improvement.

This is a great case because it's so typical of what a lot of consultants face—an organization where everything seems to be going wrong, things are falling apart, and there are lots of possible targets to pursue. And professionals not taking a performance improvement approach would likely jump to some immediate conclusions, like "Let's provide executive coaching for Theo Paine," who admitted when he took the job that he wasn't that experienced, or "Let's send everyone through training on a range of topics, like safety issues, supervision, and communication skills," or "Let's build up employee engagement."

While these may initially seem like great ideas, they aren't very systematic or very business focused (I'll explain what that means in just a bit). Additionally, when things start to go wrong in an organization, it's very easy for everything to start falling apart. A bad process or conflicting targets can lead to a situation where it seems everyone is incompetent and nothing is done right. Lightgate is a classic example of an organization where a systematic and systemic approach to performance is critical—otherwise you'll end up spending valuable resources on issues that have a tangential impact.

Let's also acknowledge that it's not clear what the business priorities are. The CEO at one point talks about sales being down, at another point about the need to speed up delivery, and a third time about the importance of reducing damages and rework, but Theo's initial priority was to "stabilize things down in the warehouse." Everyone is so busy slapping bandages on problems (or ducking responsibility and just continuing to do what they've always done) that you don't have a clear sense of what the business wants to achieve. Until we identify the business goals, it's hard to determine the most critical performance to focus on. That's a key element of any performance analysis—defining the goals, not just in terms of priorities but also in terms of metrics. (How much do sales need to change? How much faster do shipments need to be?)

There are a lot of dysfunctional elements to Lightgate as a business and how it operates, and it's easy to be distracted by them. None of the players have a good handle on what the problem is, so they're all acting on anecdotal evidence ("fire all the managers!" or "hire a people person" or "rearrange the warehouse layout" or "initiate safety training"). The late Geary Rummler used to say, "Pit a good person against a bad process, and the bad process will win almost every time." What is going on at Lightgate is repetitive and constant. It doesn't appear isolated to one shift (although the less experienced night shift appears to have more damage problems), or to one manager, supervisor, client, or set of products. My initial read is that there is a process problem, and in trying to cope with it, a series of workarounds—like banning smartphones, moving water fountains, and so forth—have compounded the issues.

So, to me, there are two main problems. First, there is no clearly enunciated business goal or way to measure it. It's as if the target keeps shifting, or the business goal is "make the pain stop!" Second, no one seems to know the root cause they're trying to address, so every action is simply a bandage based on anecdotal information. Because of these two factors, you have a

> **"Pit a good person against a bad process, and the bad process will win almost every time."**

dysfunctional organization where key processes have broken down, resulting in poor performance in almost every area (slow turnaround times, damaged products, safety violations, and so on).

Any approach to these problems has to start with the CEO. I'd first want Callaway to commit to a business priority and identify how to measure progress. Then, for whatever business goal the CEO names as top priority, I'd want to see how performance has changed over time. For instance, if the goal involves reducing waste and damaged products, I'd want to see how this is measured and look at long-term damages rates. This could tell me if the change in results correlates with a specific change in process, procedure, or internal operation. Given the turnover in operations managers, I think it's quite likely that changes in internal standard operating procedures are a factor, or that with the turnover in ops managers, some key processes or functions have fallen by the wayside.

I'm never against asking people for their opinion—it gives you the opportunity to find out what they think and sometimes provides useful insights. But to be clear: Just because everyone says "we need new equipment" or "we need more training" doesn't mean it's true. You're asking for their input partially for political reasons (so they're more likely to accept your recommendations) and because people occasionally tell you the answer to the problem. But the best approach is to use data where possible and show impact—especially for performance issues.

What are my recommendations for Theo Paine? First of all, he needs to stop trying to solve everything and stop using superficial fixes. Second, anything he can do that is a quick "win," even if it's small, will help to build credibility. Third, he's not going to be able to tackle any major organizational performance issue unless he partners with key people. That's why a "win" or good data matter—he can use them to get support and buy-in for his initiatives.

Theo would find the DNA Desktop tools from ATD's Analysis course helpful. Process maps are also very useful, especially if you're looking at how one process affects others or has a force multiplier effect. Systems theory would also help. Lightgate is a complex company with a series of feedback loops that encourage specific behaviors (such as not worrying if you break supplies or slow the delivery of products) and other loops that discourage particular behaviors (such as safety). If you understand how the system works and have the feedback loops in place, then you can start predicting results and behavior patterns. And you also identify the pressure points to go after to change the system and alter the results.

This is absolutely a common scenario. Lightgate would benefit from a systematic approach and a clear set of priorities—yet neither currently exists. The failure to have one, let alone both, results in a lot of frustration and wasted effort. It creates an atmosphere where everything feels like it's broken, and management is playing Whack-A-Mole as they react to each new problem that suddenly emerges.

TAKE 2

Commentary by Ben Locwin

Ben Locwin is CEO of a healthcare consulting organization. He has held executive roles for top pharmaceutical companies and developed human performance models for a variety of organizations.

As with any business, there are multivariate issues at play simultaneously at Lightgate that are affecting the inputs and outputs of all processes. Getting to the heart of the most influential components takes good, structured analysis and experience.

Most fundamentally, processes are the problem within Lightgate. There are so many operations occurring without standard operating procedures that it's unlikely any one employee knows exactly what to do in a repeatable way.

In addition, E.B. Callaway is unaware of how his organization is falling behind its competitors. Without a good external market analysis, it's rather unhelpful to randomly try to eliminate old initiatives or commence new ones. If the company is lagging in public perception, then he needs to fix it through initiatives that address that particular problem. If it's a problem of sales of a particular product, Callaway needs countermeasures to be more competitive in that area. Differentiation of operational strategy keeps the company focused on practical improvements to its business model, without wasting resources on random fixes. It needs to be systematic.

The case study notes that "lighting companies are increasingly joining up with IT to create smart solutions for a variety of uses. . . . It's uncertain if a company like Lightgate can adapt and thrive in this new atmosphere." There's no guarantee of Lightgate surviving just because it "wants" to. However, if it changes in an agile way to keep up with new market demands and consumer preferences, then it has a chance of surviving. There is a saying popularly attributed to W. Edwards Deming: "Change is not necessary. Survival is not mandatory."

It appears that the CEO is concerned about what things he may "need" to do to turn around revenue. Unfortunately, these tend to be short-sighted actions for short-term gains, like employee layoffs, and will never result in a long-term or sustainable strategy. Instead of looking at margins and employees as part of COGS (cost of goods sold), he should be considering how to best utilize his staff to meet the new product and service offerings that are necessary to survive in the market. Furthermore, his reasoning for hiring Theo in the first place suggests he is either a very visionary or very inexperienced CEO. Theo doesn't have the depth of experiences to draw upon for sustainable gains, but certainly could be good for an initial shift in process and employee performance.

"Change is not necessary. Survival is not mandatory."

One thing Theo needs to do is rapidly implement the 5S organization methodology in the warehouse and all operational areas. In this strategy, each S represents a step in the process for streamlining operations: sort, set in order, shine, standardize, and sustain (BPI 2014). It's a subset of lean production methods and gives employees guidance on how to improve performance, take pride in their workplace, and generate competitive performance for sustainable gains.

There's also evidence of not paying enough interest to developing staff to improve their performance. Theo's program for developing employees through on-the-job training is a good way to minimize interperson variation in performing repeated work processes. However, it remains to be seen if Evie, who is in charge of the training programs, will agree to the change.

Another major recommendation that I'd advocate for is a willingness to "trystorm" at the company. This is like brainstorming better ways of doing things, but you actually require fixes be implemented. You won't lose anything by creating pilot operational studies—if they don't work, you undo them and try something else. But, if they work, you've just improved the business's operations, and likely by a substantial amount.

On-site safety is another huge problem—safety-related negligence alone can shut a business down. There needs to be a concerted effort to fix the safety program at Lightgate. Creating key performance indicators and a safety culture that starts with leadership shows the employees that good safety procedures are nondiscretionary. This may come at the expense of some staff who don't want to adopt the new behaviors, but better the loss of incompatible staff than loss of staff due to injury or death. Reductions in recordable accidents and incidents of 90 percent or greater are achievable. It all comes down to developing rational goals, and using data-based decision making to determine the problems' root causes. Then, address the root causes systematically and systemically so that they are removed or mitigated by better processes, rather than having people be more vigilant, which never works for long-term safety incident prevention.

As for a smartphone policy, Theo can address the managers if he chooses, emphasizing that if it's important to the managers, it's important to the employees. However, he also needs to remember that managers have different jobs, and there doesn't have to be an equivalent policy for all staff in the building with respect to phones, breaks, and so forth. That's also part of the next generation of successors aspiring to move up the ranks to get different privileges.

Here are a few additional recommendations for the organization:

- Devise a better system for analytics to determine the best- and worst-selling items, SKUs to be omitted, and which item types are most often damaged. This will help develop targeted improvements so the company stops wasting time and resources on underselling items, and can get a handle on its inventory shrinkage and breakage. Creating a Pareto chart (a specialized type of bar chart that can easily highlight quality-related factors) of the most damaged items could pinpoint the likely periods when damage occurs.

- Make employees accountable for breakage that occurs on their watch. There could be deeper root causes leading to breakage, such as insufficient packaging supports and foam to protect the materials. However, if that's the case, address it by contacting product manufacturers directly. If the cause is careless handling, then a daily accountability board—with names—will stop material loss almost immediately. Nothing works better than public accountability in an insular work environment. Continuous recidivism can be dealt with by termination, but only if there's reckless and willful neglect or gross incompetence that has been addressed previously by training initiatives.

- There appear to be serious personality issues throughout the hierarchy at Lightgate. They may be just as influential as the systemic issues and process issues within the company. Theo needs to be given the empowerment and jurisdiction to execute his role. And his work should include focusing on process more than "superheroes"—cultivating the soon-to-be retired Sam Winston, for example—and nonrepeatable performances. This will reduce variation and make the business much more predictable and profitable.

2

"DID YOU READ THE MEMO?"

Cast of Characters at the New Leaf Foundation

Neil Proctor—Advancement Director
Meredith Marks—Major Gifts Officer, Reports to Neil
Cara James—CEO
Jane Brady—Meredith's Assistant

Meredith Marks had more than a decade of experience in fundraising strategy and donor cultivation when she was recruited to be the major gifts officer in the New Leaf Foundation's development office. Prior to working for New Leaf, Meredith headed up the alumni foundation office at Shepherd College, where she had acquired some large and noteworthy donations.

Meredith had just returned from a grueling five-day trip of home visits with several donors, combined with two media events. Her travel schedule was always heavy this time of year, but she was in touch with the office daily, at least through Jane Brady, her assistant.

Meredith's boss—Neil Proctor, the advancement director—also was often out of the office on foundation outreach. However, he usually took days to respond to emails of any kind. Jane had complained to her that Neil's frequent absences made it difficult to get basic approvals reviewed and signed. And she'd told Meredith that lately people had begun calling him the "memo king."

"You're joking, right?"

"No, he prefers memos to emails."

"When is an email just an email?"

"When it doesn't say memo."

＊　＊　＊

For the past few months, Neil had been busy with a rebranding initiative, and a clutch of consultants often encircled him when he was in the office. Meredith hadn't seen any specifics of Neil's plan—she'd only heard that it would set the foundation on a new course, modernizing both its projected public face and its internal structure and communications.

Part of the plan was creating a new logo. Meredith wondered what was so wrong with the existing one—based on a botanical print of the 19th-century illustrator Alois Auer. She thought it captured the foundation's mission uniting nature and culture; it was both simple and elegant. Maybe it wasn't a huge matter, she thought, but it was definitely a symbolic one.

Neither did she understand the purpose of the "new course." She had long admired the foundation's work and yearned to be a part of an institution with such a high purpose. She felt fulfilled in her development work—it was aligned with New Leaf's mission, all was well, and no new course was needed.

Her best guess was that Neil's plans had something to with the building proposal from CEO Cara James, which the foundation's board of directors had approved a year ago. The foundation had spread out over the years from its small, appealing center near Shepherd College to a leafy block of neighboring townhouses. Meredith thought the location kept the foundation friendly, accessible, and close to its mission and the heart of its work. But the new building would be built on undeveloped riverfront land that was five miles outside town.

The New Leaf Foundation

The New Leaf Foundation is an independent nonprofit charitable organization dedicated to assisting local communities with social issues of concern—from employment, housing, domestic violence, and immigration to environmental pollutants, rural development, and water quality. The foundation is well respected by the broad range of community groups it serves, the federal and local government entities with whom it works, and the general public, who trusts the foundation as a reliable neighbor. Founded in 1948 by an anonymous benefactor and with a current net worth of about $125 million, it is popular with many along the political spectrum, established in the capital, and has a strong statewide reputation and volunteer base. Its stated mission is "to serve the public good by positively affecting social welfare and supporting community life in all its forms."

The New Leaf Foundation's 16-member board of directors, drawn from both the local community and across the country, meets quarterly, with its powerful, six-member executive committee meeting monthly. But little is known about the foundation's inner workings or how it manages day-to-day operations at its main headquarters, where it employs about 200 people. Its reputation and mission makes it an attractive employer across its departments, which focus on public initiatives, grantmaking and development, communications, finance, and administration. If there was little transparency, there also seemed to be little need for public scrutiny.

Failing to Ask

Cara, a former high-profile economics professor and the author of a well-reviewed book on the history of social causes and economic policy, had taken over as the director and CEO of New Leaf when the much-loved former CEO, who was trusted by the board, retired. She was often pulled into planning meetings for the new building, but the fundraising typically fell to Meredith, who couldn't help but note that there was no budget approval for the building and Cara had not yet approached anyone on the board for a major gift. When the board approved Cara's plan, she'd had them in the room—all of them, face to face—and yet asked for nothing. They needed to raise millions, and Meredith felt she was being asked to do all of it herself. Most CEOs had a better understanding of their fundraising role.

At the first New Leaf all-staff meeting when Cara announced her plans for the new building, she seemed surprised by the level of employee resistance. She was eager to share the site plan, with a building footprint twice the size of their present one, and light-filled open space and conference rooms, but she was unprepared to answer the simple question of why this was happening now. How would it affect the foundation's regular program work and projected funding requests? After all, the previous CEO had already drafted a modernizing plan, so said a friendly board member. Cara now wondered if her predecessor chose to retire rather than even attempt to change a popular strategic course of action.

Meanwhile, Neil had yet to schedule a staff meeting about the rebranding or the new logo because of his travel schedule; instead, he offered memo updates, which many staff ignored. Meredith found herself thinking fondly of her last position, where she held weekly prospect meetings with her staff; although she met with Jane and her New Leaf staff weekly, she simply emailed her updates to Neil.

On the one hand, Meredith viewed Cara's and Neil's remoteness as an expression of their confidence in her abilities; on the other hand, she worried that they were simply inattentive to, or out of touch with, the foundation, its business, and staff.

For weeks, Meredith had been trying to connect Cara with an important prospective donor who had a specific funding interest that would need her special attention. Meredith had lucked into the tip on her last trip, when one of her favorite donors described a certain friend's passion for classical music education—which also happened to be a new middle-school funding initiative of the foundation's. When Meredith learned who that friend was, a certain celebrity chef who had the same New York publisher as her CEO, she thought the ask was as good as done. She was excited—these discoveries were the little veins of gold that fundraisers toiled to mine; no amount of traditional wealth analysis could uncover them.

Meredith knew what her job was in these situations—prepare and set the way for the meeting, which would occur at the highest level. She had no problem with that. Some prospective donors were specific about only wanting CEO contact, while others appreciated Meredith's efforts and simply followed her lead to Cara. But Cara was another matter. These days, she seemed distracted, unavailable, and rarely alone.

Neil and Cara

"Time for lunch today?"

"Is that a meal or a concept?"

"The former, and unfamiliarity with it breeds starvation."

"How about 1, our usual place?"

* * *

Again, Meredith tried to follow up with Cara, but by the end of the week she still hadn't heard from her and wondered if she was out of town. She hadn't seen anything that would indicate that in the staff schedule, but perhaps it was an impromptu trip. The prospective donor was now traveling as well, and while she'd replied to Meredith's early overtures after their chance meeting, she, too, was now unresponsive. Meredith decided to approach Neil.

"I've got a great opportunity for us and need your help with Cara."

"Sure. Is it for the capital campaign?"

"Umm, could be."

"Well, that'd be great. She's been trying to get some of the board to sign on, and they've been very slow to support us. So anything we can do more publicly would be welcome."

"I'll see what I can do, but first if you could get me in with her, I'd appreciate it. She seems quite busy."

"Later on tonight, stop by the board meeting. You know some of them anyway."

The Board Meets

When the board of directors approved Cara's building plan a year ago, some members pointed out that her chosen site, an undeveloped riverfront property, had environmental restrictions and wasn't appropriate for an organization with New Leaf's mission. Cara suggested that with the appropriate design, the building could be dramatic, compelling, and lead to further protection of the riverfront area. Others pointed out that the foundation wasn't a conservation group per se, that other groups with such a mission could better protect the 20-acre parcel, or perhaps partner with New Leaf, but Cara won out and secured approval for the land purchase outright, for $17 million, from a former board member.

At that same meeting, the board was introduced to Neil, the new director of advancement, who delivered a presentation for updating the logo. Some of the board, particularly those who had been part of the current logo's selection years ago with the former CEO, didn't understand or agree with Neil's reasoning. They still identified the organization with the previous CEO and her mission, and didn't feel the need for change. Other board members who had come on since Cara's arrival were entrepreneurial, vocal, and persuasive in welcoming Neil's modernizing views and direction. Neil, trying to be conciliatory, promised to arrange a meeting with the board and the advertising firm he had chosen to design the prospective logo. But then, some board members, who were also on the powerful executive committee, wondered why there hadn't been more discussion first rather than the presentation of a fait accompli.

Sensing an opening, Neil didn't wait for the next quarterly board meeting. Instead, he went to the executive committee meeting later that month with the principals of the design firm in tow. Together, they presented several rebranding options to the committee and entertained their suggestions and addressed their concerns. This action angered many of the board members not on the executive committee, who pointed out that the purpose of the smaller group was to do the business of the board, but not act independently of it. While they had certainly heard of this kind of friction developing between other boards and committees, it had never been the nature of the New Leaf Foundation board.

The following two quarterly meetings were fully and, some observed, tensely attended.

* * *

Meredith didn't feel like going to the board meeting. She'd heard about the recent friction caused by the logo and building proposals and the unexpected retirement of a few highly regarded program heads. She wasn't sure it was the place for her, but she wanted to get a moment with Cara.

That evening, after Jane popped in to say goodnight and the rest of the floor was quiet, Meredith headed up to the sixth floor to Cara's office suite. She knocked softly, opened the outer door—and startled Cara and Neil, heads together, deep in conversation.

Recovering quickly, Neil said, "Come on in. We were just getting ready to go over to the board meeting. Join us."

Meredith didn't respond, but stood in the doorway and watched as Cara, now scrolling through her phone, suddenly looked in her direction, smiled, and extended her hand in welcome. "Yes, you should come with us."

Now Meredith realized she wouldn't get time to speak to Cara about her donor after all. She had never heard any talk of anything between Neil and Cara, and while it was hard for her to keep up on relationships in the organization given how much she traveled, this one still would have taken some effort to hide. When Neil was hired last year, there been some criticism of his qualifications as overly academic and without much foundation experience, yet others thought his Ivy League background would be an asset. Did Cara know Neil from when they were both academics? She had never heard mention of a prior relationship. But now Meredith wondered whether her boss was declining to back her funding requests as he sought support for his own. Was he competing with her?

A Prior Relationship

When the local newspaper story about the foundation's financial troubles first appeared, many in the community were surprised, even those long acquainted with New Leaf. How could an organization with such strong donor support and financial prospects have an annual deficit growing well into the millions?

According to financial analysts, Cara's modernizing infrastructure and building mission was proving both extravagant and underfunded, risking grantmaking and sustaining programs. What's more, there were unattributed quotes from longtime board members pointing to conflicts of interest in the land purchase, as well as a prior relationship between the CEO and the advancement director.

* * *

"You didn't know?"

"I didn't, but it's starting to make sense."

"How so?"

"She'd been so distracted. Out of touch."

"No, I think she is very focused. Driven in fact. Just not in the same way as you."

TAKE 1

Commentary by Tom Kaiden

*Tom Kaiden is the chief operating officer of Visit Alexandria,
in Alexandria, Virginia.*

This case raises the question, "What can you do as a middle manager
when there is poor leadership at the top?"

Until recently, the New Leaf Foundation had enjoyed a strong
reputation as a bulwark of the community. But there's clearly trou-
ble afoot. Cara, the newly appointed CEO, just spent $17 million
to buy land for a new building, with board approval, but without a
budget or development plan for the building itself. Cara has a fundraising background, yet seems suddenly unwilling to participate in the
core fundraising aspect of her job. The organization is now running
a multimillion-dollar deficit. The board is divided over the organization's new direction. Senior leaders are leaving the organization. There
is little transparency from, or accessibility to, the leadership team.
With leadership failure on many fronts, this is an organization on the
brink of crisis.

Both Cara and Neil are diverting resources (time, money, people)
into their pet projects—a new building and a rebranding effort—
which both seem unnecessary. As a reader, I'd love to say that this case
is unrealistic, because who would do that? But sadly, situations like this
are more common than we would like to admit. New executives, senior
leaders, and board members often believe that they have a mandate
for change, and so will look for a project on which they can put their

stamp. Buildings and rebranding campaigns are common examples of such projects. It would be great to think that because nonprofits are mission driven, they are immune from excess, but there are plenty of examples of executive hubris in communities all across the country.

So, what is Meredith to do?

In the short-term, she should accept Cara and Neil's invitation to walk with them to the board meeting. She needs to expressly ask Cara to join her on the call to the prospective donor for middle-school music education funding. And then she needs to get that date on Cara's calendar. Meredith seems reluctant to join Cara and Neil, because of both the imminent timing of the board meeting and the perception of a personal relationship between them. But this is the moment she has access, so she needs to use it. And Cara and Neil's relationship is speculative and irrelevant.

Beyond this short-term situation, there is another reason Meredith needs to attend the board meeting. The board is the key to righting the ship at New Leaf. The members are currently divided, and Meredith, for her own career security, should take this opportunity to assess the board's appetite and capacity to rein in the CEO. Boards are often reluctant to insist on executive change, particularly if the leader is so new in tenure. This case is complicated by the board's complicity in approving the land purchase without a budget for construction or a development plan to pay for it.

It's said that the first rule of holes is, "When you're in one, stop digging." If I were Meredith, I would want to determine how likely the board is to step in and demand a course correction. She has an opportunity in this moment to see them in action, and she should take it.

If the board seems divided and hesitant to act, she should look at updating her resume and exploring other options. A major gifts officer is highly dependent on an active CEO to achieve her goals. In this

> It's said that the first rule of holes is, "When you're in one, stop digging."

case, Meredith lacks the attention and participation of the advancement officer and CEO, which will make her job impossible. Moreover, the organization is moving rapidly from a position of strength to one of financial instability and mission drift. On this current course, there is a high likelihood that Meredith will be tarnished by the organization's reputational fall, so getting out sooner rather than later makes sense. Given the similar actions taken by other senior leaders, the best career path forward might be an immediate change.

Certainly, no organization, job, leader, or employee is perfect. The question for all of us is whether we have the authority and resources for positive change within our current role. When external forces beyond our control have mounted to such an extent that we cannot overcome them, then job change is the rational path forward. That's the issue that Meredith must ultimately address.

TAKE 2

Commentary by Alan De Back

Alan De Back is a career counselor and learning consultant with more than 20 years of experience. He has served as director of global learning for an Internet consulting firm and manager of leadership development for a major aerospace corporation.

Change is constant, but it can become a major issue if the reasons for change are not clearly explained. Within both the organization and the community, any communication must deliver a clear and consistent message. With a nonprofit organization like New Leaf, change is even more difficult. The foundation has experienced major changes in leadership, and the new strategies being implemented were not clearly articulated or understood.

The issues here are directly related to communication (both internal and external) and with trying to make major changes to an established organizational culture.

Meredith is struggling with her desire to do an exceptional job in fundraising without the access to leadership that she needs. She clearly understands how to do her job effectively, but needs regular communication with both Neil and Cara. And her consistent attempts to communicate with both have not been successful.

Neil and Cara don't appear to be communicating regularly or consistently with the foundation's staff. When Cara held the all-staff meeting about the proposed new building, she seemed totally surprised by the questions and resistance from staff members. She isolated herself, and had no idea how they would react to the new strategies being implemented.

Neil has yet to meet with the staff to discuss his rebranding ideas. Although they are the ones who will need to support and execute his plans, he has only sent them memo updates. He very much needs to communicate in a way that will get his team on board to support him in implementing the changes.

Change is constant, but it can become a major issue if the reasons are not clearly explained.

External communications also have been inconsistent and often inappropriate. Neil's presentation of rebranding options to the executive committee was not well received by other board members who weren't present at the meeting. Friction within the board, and between the board and Cara's team, will create other issues. And a story in the local newspaper about the foundation's financial problems opened a door to the community about what was happening internally.

And let's not forget that Neil and Cara appear to have had a previous (and current?) relationship that many within the foundation suspect. If this relationship does exist, it needs to be addressed.

Clearly, new approaches to communication within the foundation are critical.

First, the foundation should hire a communications director immediately. That person needs to be given authority to oversee both internal and external communication. Internal communication needs to flow with transparency if staff members are going to support both the rebranding and the construction of the new building. External communications also need to be controlled to ensure clarity and consistency. A good communications director can build solid relationships with the media in the community, and could help control a story like the one that appeared in the local paper. Without a person in this role, communication will continue to be ad hoc and the messaging unclear.

Additionally, both Cara and Neil need to better understand the importance of appropriate, regular communication. They are both so involved in the changes that they want to implement that they have forgotten that the most critical element of change management is clear, consistent messaging. Cara would not have been so surprised by the reaction at the staff meeting if she had been regularly communicating with and listening to her staff.

If there is a relationship between Neil and Cara, they need to make a decision as to whether Neil's continued employment at the foundation is feasible. If the relationship is causing a conflict of interest with the work he is doing, Neil should resign.

As for Meredith, she needs to assertively insist on more regular communication with both Neil and Cara. She appears to be attempting to meet with them both on an as-needed basis, but that approach is not working. They are not available when she needs them, and she doesn't have the information she needs to do her job. She also knows that Neil prefers to communicate by "memo," so she may want to consider adjusting her communication mode to accommodate his preferences. The case study does not make clear how flexible Meredith has been in choosing her modes of communication.

Without regular communication, Meredith's ability to do her job is greatly diminished. Her effectiveness is critical to the foundation's financial solvency. If Meredith is unable to get the consistent meetings and communication with both Neil and Cara, she needs to make a decision about her future with the foundation. She should prepare a transition plan for herself if she can't get the support she needs, and be prepared to implement that plan and move on to a different organization.

3

DRIVING THE BUS

Cast of Characters at nFold

Diana David—Software Engineer, Manager of a Small Team

Nell Sturgis—Quality Engineer on Diana's Team

Patrick, Kent, Wes, and Saeed—Programmers on Diana's Team

Drew West—Former Manager of Diana's Team

Diana David was a talented software engineer. She was also a manager, with little experience, leading a team at nFold, a rapidly growing tech startup. Her first manager had confided to her that to achieve team success, "Get the right people on the bus and the wrong people off." Now that she was in charge, however, Diana was finding that easier said than done.

Diana's new team had five people: a quality engineer, Nell Sturgis, and four programmers, Patrick, Kent, Wes, and Saeed. The programmers all had graduate degrees from top schools and had been working with one another for several scrums now. They were under a lot of pressure to produce in quite complex projects, and as a result could be intense and questioning of one another. Diana also thought they too easily crossed the line to challenge her in meetings.

"I often feel like I have to prove myself to them," she'd told Drew, the former team manager, shortly after she'd taken over. The team needed the high performers, to be sure, but Diana also needed them to be open and accepting.

In addition, Nell was struggling to keep up. In fact, Drew had warned Diana that Nell needed a performance improvement plan.

"Honestly, these plans usually don't improve employee performance," he said. "More often than not, they demoralize the individual, compelling them to quit, but I don't think the team has another choice. The wrong person on a team can make everyone less productive; the wrong person can lower the bar for everyone."

Diana knew that the bus analogy was often quoted among business students and managers. Yet she wondered if it aptly described her circumstances and who she was. Was it possible for the bus to slow down for passengers who needed a change in speed or direction? She was starting to think that it wasn't. And, didn't greatness sometimes take time to develop? This question also nagged at her as she considered the ultra-competitive world she now worked in, her new team, and what it would take to make them successful.

Toxic Early Culture

There was no mistaking that Diana was now in her dream job—a startup software company specializing in cloud-based solutions. She was drawn to the organization's ambitious mission and creative environment. But it had taken her some time to get there.

A promising career start, after graduating at the top of her college class, was followed by several years at a large nonprofit organization providing evaluation and research services to client entities. The physical environment at the nonprofit was all hushed hallways, closed doors, and walls, and Diana had few opportunities to collaborate with her fellow team members. She could go for a whole day without talking to anyone.

Managers often seemed tense, and one, who had 60 direct reports, was known to yell in meetings, stomp off, and swear behind people's backs. Diana didn't know much about leadership, but she knew it didn't look like that.

Even though she didn't always find the work challenging or interesting, Diana gave 100 percent and received high performance evaluations. Yet the isolation and toxic management wore her down; she was miserable without knowing why.

After nearly a decade with the company (an unusual tenure in technology), Diana was promoted to manage a team for the first time. Her immediate supervisor, who was a social scientist and not a programmer, relied on her technical skill, and she began to flourish in this relationship. But before long, she began to wonder if her success, although deserved, was simply masking a poor working culture and keeping her from finding a better fit. She worried about becoming not better and more experienced with age, but diminished and unable to keep up technically. She had no career development plan and no mentor. At that point, she reached out to a coach.

And soon after, she left for nFold.

From Quiet to Chaos

Founded five years ago, nFold made a quick product splash with an easy, affordable solution for project-sharing software. Since then, it had emerged from its much-hailed infancy to grow steadily and stand on its own. Now, the addition of a new set of customer care products set the company in line for an initial public stock offering, hiring was picking up organization wide, and three regional offices were being added.

Diana's new team worked in an open-office plan, with desks grouped in two parallel rows. Everyone had a standing desk, and while there wasn't much personal space, there was plenty of social interaction. Snacks and meals were brought in, and people worked. It all contributed to engagement at a much higher level than Diana was accustomed to, or, she thought, existed at a traditional workplace. She noted that people seemed to work basically every minute they were in the office, and often worked from home in the evenings without being asked. Many staff set their own work arrangements; Diana could work from home if she chose to, but she never did because, for her, the workplace was finally exciting.

But it could also be chaotic and distracting. Sometimes Diana had to use noise-canceling headphones to help herself think; she'd also occasionally go to the library or duck into an empty conference room.

Who Belongs on the Bus?

While Nell wasn't as technically proficient as the others, Diana thought her main problem was actually time management; perhaps the hectic, demanding schedule was contributing to her struggles. So when Drew recommended implementing a performance plan, she thought of offering Nell a plan that focused on accuracy, not speed.

"I identify with Nell," she'd said. "That could have been me. I never had a mentor. No one on the job ever advised or coached me."

But before offering Nell the performance improvement plan, Diana invited her to lunch. When they met, Nell was ready with her own plan.

"I'd like to become a programmer."

"Do you need a mentor?"

"Are you offering?"

"I am."

"And how would that work?"

"Any way you want. If you'd like, we could see about transferring you to another team so you're not reporting directly to me."

Nell considered the offer, then quickly changed the subject. "You know, the guys talk over each other, and they talk over you. They're so lacking in respect."

"It's not perfect," admitted Diana. "It's a challenge to lead a team."

"If I were a developer, it might be no different."

"Maybe not, but teams are all different. You could try another. Or, maybe another kind of employer. I came from a very traditional place, more of a research culture, all offices with doors."

"Sounds like heaven," Nell said dreamily.

"Just make sure you don't overcorrect."

* * *

After lunch, Nell went back to her desk to think about her options. She had a few—seek a mentor, transfer to another team, try to get training to become a developer—but now she had to decide which was the most realistic.

As Diana reflected on her lunch with Nell, she realized that in the excitement of hearing Nell's plan, she hadn't shared her performance improvement plan. Nell seemed to like Diana's idea to mentor her, but now Diana wondered if she was being too hasty. Maybe she should have shared her plan after all.

TAKE 1

Commentary by Vivian Blade

Vivian Blade is a talent management strategist, author, keynote speaker, leadership development trainer, and executive coach.

Diana is dealing with several challenges, including her own leadership experience and capacity, the organizational culture, dynamics within her team, and individual personnel.

Her inexperience as a leader is hindering her team's progress. In addition, Diana's early exposure to poor leadership has shaped her leadership style—mostly from lessons learned that she will not do. Her current company, having recently transitioned from a startup to a growing, larger organization, isn't a good role model of leadership for its growth structure either. Diana's lack of formal leadership development is compounded because she doesn't have a mentor to give feedback and share other perspectives. So, Diana is left to make her own judgments on what she observes, and doesn't fully understand her role. She recognizes that some things need to change, but doesn't know what she should be doing to establish and lead a high-performing team.

While Diana is so focused on "having the right people on the bus in the right seat," she doesn't realize she needs to look at the design and health of the bus itself.

The team's working relationships are more competitive than supportive, which may stem from a lack of trust within the team. Because the culture did not evolve as the company grew from the start-up stage, the programmers, who have been around since its infancy, continue to work in a small, entrepreneurial cultural style. Organizational values, behaviors, and team norms were not established as the company grew. If they were defined, they didn't filter down through the organization. The four programmers know one another well and are used to working together. However, the addition of a new leader and quality engineer disrupted their norms. They also may be feeling some loss of autonomy.

Additionally, Diana needs to assess whether Nell is in the right position. Are the team dynamics and work process keeping her from being successful? During the lunch conversation, Diana avoided having a frank discussion with Nell. Instead, she used Nell's idea for her career change as a distraction from addressing real development opportunities. She didn't provide any guidance for how Nell might think about the right move for herself. And, she didn't give any direction for how the mentoring process would work.

Diana doesn't realize she needs to look at the design and health of the bus itself.

Diana's overall goal should be to become a better leader, working with her team to create an environment where they can effectively contribute to the company's growth. What actions should Diana take to manage the current challenges and achieve these outcomes? Let's first address the most pressing needs and where she has direct control.

Often, an organization's infrastructure does not effectively support the work a team needs to accomplish. This is one of the first places leaders should look as they assess the outcomes of their team. First, Diana needs to evaluate her "bus," and then she can assess the roles needed and determine whether her current team members meet those needs. These questions will help her determine gaps and priorities:

- What is the team's purpose and function? What deliverables are expected?

- Are functional processes and systems defined, in place, and followed to support her team's deliverables?
- Is the organizational structure set up to work effectively toward meeting her team's purpose, function, and deliverables?
- Are the job function and accountabilities for each role well defined?
- Has she defined the technical and soft skills required for success for each role?
- Have expectations been clearly set and communicated to each employee?
- Have employees received the training required to be successful in their roles?
- Is the team culture inclusive and engaging? Do employees work together as a team toward a common goal? Are working relationships constructive?

One of a leader's most important roles is building a high-functioning team. It appears that some foundation setting did not take place as Diana stepped into this role. Even though the team seems to have established some undesirable norms, she can engage them in intentionally redefining their goals and norms collectively. These steps and tools will help her lead this effort:

- Engage the team in defining their vision and setting team goals. This will build personal ownership among team members.
- Give the team a sense of purpose by connecting the importance of their work to achieving the vision for the company.
- Share observations and concerns about the team's working relationships and how that affects their outcomes. Have team members share their observations and concerns, too.
- Engage the team in defining their working relationships, values, and team norms. Ensure their roles and responsibilities are defined and understood across the team. Why are all

roles important? Agree that challenging each other can be constructive; however, make sure that all are on board with the basic approach.

- Use an assessment such as Myers-Briggs or DiSC to understand team members' personalities, interaction styles, and work preferences. Review results with the team and provide strategies on how to effectively work together.
- An assessment such as Patrick Lencioni's *Five Dysfunctions of a Team* can also be a resource to uncover some of their underlying issues.
- Work on building trust within the team. Diana can model trust and earn trust by ensuring she leads with integrity, communicates frequently and honestly, and demonstrates respect for her team's expertise and experience. *The Trust Edge* (2009) can guide her through author David Horsager's eight pillars of trust within her team.

As for Nell, Diana should more carefully assess her direct report's performance before deciding if a performance improvement plan is warranted. It appears that her personal observations did not align with her predecessor's opinion. Diana should consider whether a combination of organizational and personal factors may be playing a role in Nell's performance. As she assesses these factors, she should objectively consider the following questions and associated tools that can help her:

- Have expectations been clearly set and communicated to Nell? How does her performance compare against those expectations?
- Assess whether Nell has the skills and training required for the role using tools like the SHL Software Quality Assurance Skills Test.
- Assess how Nell's strengths and interests match those required by the job using tools such as StrengthsFinder, CliftonStrengths, or the SHL Occupational Personality Profile.

- Is Nell giving full effort to her role? How is her attendance? Does she seem interested and engaged in her work?

Additionally, Diana should talk with Nell to get her perspective on what she thinks the challenges are and why. Are there some things that Nell can take responsibility for to improve the situation? They can discuss how Nell might have greater success in her current role, and how some of the team's ideas are being implemented to improve the team culture. Nell currently has no career plan, and she doesn't know if the roles she is looking at would be a better fit for her. Using the insights from the assessments, Diana and a mentor can work with Nell to develop a career plan and evaluate what might be the best fit for her inside or outside her organization. She should introduce Nell to the book *Find Your Fit* (Kaiden 2016), which references a variety of useful career resources.

Regarding her own leadership style, Diana needs to understand the many facets of leadership so that she can recognize what she hasn't been doing and needs to be doing in her role. She can work with her HR partner to enroll in a leadership development program, and may want to consider engaging an executive coach. A trusted adviser or mentor who can advise Diana in her leadership growth will be an essential resource in her development. This person may not be in her current organization.

Diana also needs feedback on her current leadership from her team, peers, senior leaders, and others who work with her. She can use tools like a 360-degree feedback or emotional intelligence assessment from resources like the Leadership Practices Inventory (LPI) Assessment, Hogan 360, Hogan EQ, or the SHL Occupational Personality Profile—Leadership.

As for the company itself, enhancements in the company's overall culture will have a positive impact on Diana's team. As organizational values, behaviors, and norms for their larger structure are defined, communicated, and modeled from the top, employees can begin to shift their personal expectations and behaviors. Employee engagement feedback and practices will help ensure that a more inclusive environment exists. Diana should share her observations about the current environment, as well as the influence on her team, with her boss and even the CEO to heighten awareness and influence change.

Many of these actions are not quick fixes. Diana can make consistent and significant progress by setting priorities and taking it a step at a time. As she learns more about her leadership role and gains additional experience, the actions she needs to take will become more intuitive. Engaging the team in the process will increase ownership and engagement, as well as accelerate the team's success.

TAKE 2

Commentary by Alan De Back

Alan De Back is a career counselor and learning consultant with more than 20 years of experience. He has served as director of global learning for an Internet consulting firm and manager of leadership development for a major aerospace corporation.

Diana's issues are not uncommon in young, rapidly growing technology organizations. Because of the rapid growth, the managerial and support mechanisms are often not in place to support either managers or employees. Thus, the major problems in this scenario are both individual and organizational.

First, Diana is relatively inexperienced as a manager. Although her intentions are great, she has not been given the knowledge or tools to fill her role effectively. Diana also appears to either be receiving no support from her management, or she has not asked for it. If her manager does have the resources to assist her, she should be reaching out and asking for help. Without training in managerial skills and strategies or support from leadership, she will continue to struggle as a manager.

Diana also has gone through an overwhelming change in corporate culture. Her old organization and her new one have completely opposite cultures. Although she articulated that she wanted a more collaborative atmosphere and a more open work environment, she seems to be having difficulty adjusting to an extreme example of what she thought she wanted.

I would recommend that Diana work with a coach to assess whether she is in an environment where she can succeed. She was working with a coach when she made the decision to move to nFold, and she should do so again. If she determines that the nFold culture is right for her, what steps can she take to better function in that environment? If not, what does she need to do to move to an organization with a culture and environment that are a better fit for her?

Diana has gone through an overwhelming change in corporate culture.

If Diana stays, she needs training in more effective managerial strategies. Although her team sounds very bright and motivated, they appear to be forging ahead with little direction. While continuing to support the open and collaborative environment, Diana needs the tools to rein in the team a bit and provide the direction and guidance they are lacking.

These strategies would also help Diana rethink her overall approach to Nell's performance. Because Diana identifies so strongly with Nell, she has ignored Nell's issues with technical proficiency. Her focus on soft skills like time management is problematic if Nell actually does lack the technical skills she needs to succeed. Diana also jumped way too quickly to offer to be Nell's mentor. At this point, she is not the right person to fill that role, and it would necessitate changes in organizational structure. In addition, Diana's own issues make her a less-than-ideal mentor candidate.

I would recommend that rather than putting Nell on a performance plan, Diana work with her on an individual development plan (IDP) focused on her technical proficiency. Nell appears to have a positive attitude, and an IDP would provide much more incentive to develop her skills than a performance plan.

As for nFold, it appears to be struggling with managerial issues, as is the case with many young organizations. Diana is probably typical of many managers, who are hired or promoted primarily because of their technical expertise. There is no evidence of either training or adequate managerial support for someone like her.

Because the environment at nFold is so open and dynamic, there also seem to be issues with teams working together effectively. Again, there is no evidence of training or support in teamwork or team dynamics. nFold should probably take a hard look at their organizational structure and how their organization is functioning. They seem to be focusing primarily on growth, and that growth may be out of control.

I would further recommend that nFold consider bringing in an outside organization development (OD) consultant to analyze their overall situation. With so much focus on growth, management appears to have paid little attention to how the organization is functioning. They may need a neutral outside expert to advise them on the path forward. As for resources, depending on the recommendations from the OD consultant, a team-building tool or personality assessment, such as DiSC, could be useful for getting teams and their supervisors to work together more effectively. A communications self-assessment such as *What's My Communication Style?* (HRDQ 2008) could also be useful in helping team members enhance their strengths and address challenges in communicating with one another.

4

"ALL MY PEOPLE ARE GREAT"

Cast of Characters at Auruco

Nolan Landry—Longtime Manager in IT
Camila Parsons—New CTDO Appointed by CEO

Nolan Landry was a longtime manager in IT who thought all his people were great, every one of them. He'd been with Auruco for three decades, a manager for most of that time, and would tell you he had a "tough but fair" reputation around most of his direct reports. His current team of 10 varied among several specialists, a mix of newer and longtime employees, who were loaned out to different departments across the organization to fix things and troubleshoot problems. Some worked remotely.

A Company Cowboy

A few years ago, Nolan's team had come under HR scrutiny because it wasn't on an annual performance review schedule. This rankled HR, which told Nolan that he and his team should be aligned with everybody else in the organization and follow the company-wide forced distribution ranking for performance reviews. Ever since, there'd been a level of mistrust between the two.

HR had reasoned with Nolan that performance reviews were important because over the years, grade inflation by managers had become such a problem that it was difficult to identify who was a high potential and worthy of development from those who weren't. But Nolan wasn't having it. He went directly to his boss to explain the fallacy of fitting his people along a bell curve, where small percentages of people at the high and low ends were deemed "excellent" and "unsatisfactory," respectively, and a main group in the middle was "meeting requirements."

The point of these company regulations, Nolan felt, was to toughen standards for all while increasing productivity, but it basically eliminated those employees at the bottom. His people were productive, and such a system compelled him to waste time on percentages and metrics when he could be doing more important things. He could see how that effort might be worth it in a bigger department or team, where the actual numbers represented by the percentages would be larger, but to practice it on a team of 10 meant that good people would be relegated to the bottom, even when they weren't poor performers.

Ranking would also undermine his team's collaboration, he continued. Why would you take your time to help a co-worker if that might place them ahead of you? Why would you ask for help if it might lower your standing? Teamwork was essential. Besides, the staff on Nolan's team did different things, and couldn't easily be compared with one another.

Ultimately, Nolan believed, forcing out those at the bottom, although initially controlling costs, would eventually increase outsourcing until the organization realized institutional knowledge had been bled away. He had heard about competitors that had cut too close to the bone. Nolan had also heard other stories of HR departments that didn't even notice when their organization's tech talent was being recruited by an attractive competitor—until it was too late.

Nolan's boss sided with him, HR relented, and ever since the "forced distribution episode," Nolan had been viewed as a bit of a company cowboy.

For his part, Nolan didn't miss the hundreds of hours he used to spend each year writing performance reviews, but he now probably spent more time with the team and knew more about what they were doing—he had to, in order to keep up.

Instead of reviews, Nolan's team routinely met when projects were completed to discuss what happened—and what should have happened. As his team grew, from five to eight to 10, he had dispensed with the weekly one-on-ones in favor of these freewheeling post-mortems. No one seemed to miss the face-to-face chats, and the new people didn't know what they were missing. Team meetings, on the other hand, seemed useful for everybody, and those not on the specific project detail were also invited to participate, making for a lively discussion. When HR asked if they could sit in on one such discussion, Nolan politely refused. But when Camila Parsons, the company's new chief talent development officer (CTDO), approached him with the same request, Nolan thought he had to give in.

"Don't worry," Camila said. "I won't stop you and ask you to explain things for me. I'll try to come prepared."

Nolan was used to having to explain IT processes and terms to people outside the team, but found it frustrating if customers or invited guests slowed down a team meeting. However, he'd noticed that a couple of the newer team members seemed a little more deliberate about responding in meetings, and might welcome an explanatory pause to get up to speed.

A New CTDO in Town

Camila had been on the job less than a year and was still making the rounds of business-critical departments. She had been hired after

Auruco's new CEO, who was dedicated to talent acquisition and development, announced that he wanted to create more of a business partnership with HR.

Camila had never worked in such a large organization. Auruco was a multinational biotech company worth billions of dollars—an economic monolith whose biomedical research and development division alone employed more than 6,000 scientists and physicians in several locations all over the world. She was expected to develop relationships with entirely different executive teams. In this arrangement, there was both independence and responsibility. Camila was also pretty sure that, thanks to her previous job at a tech startup, the CEO had an expectation that she could promote an innovative culture in an establishment world, or at least recognize one when she saw it.

HR had brought Nolan to Camila's attention because of his perceived management problems and reluctance to set individual goals for team members, coach them, and do meaningful performance reviews. Members of Nolan's team often received positive reviews with little to no differentiation. HR thought Nolan had left them little choice.

What's more, the product line his team had been developing was stalled, and it wasn't clear if the problem was the product, the team, or its leadership.

Camila agreed with Nolan about the potential hazards and wastes of forced distribution and was relieved that the organization seemed to have moved beyond that as a personnel evaluation method. She preferred other ways to encourage productivity and motivation and cut costs. But what would work best for Nolan and his team? Coaching, reassignment, or something else?

When "How's It Going?" Isn't Enough

Camila grabbed her to-go order from the counter and motioned for Nolan to follow her. The Auruco campus sat on hundreds of green acres bordered by woods at the edge of the city research network. The day was bright and blue outside the glassed-in cafeteria, and she headed for a picnic table under a maple tree. As they sat down across from each other and unwrapped their sandwiches, Camila eyed Nolan.

"I had a manager once who used to say he could tell how engaged people were by the time of day they left work," Camila said.

"Ah, a clock-watcher," responded Nolan before biting into his sandwich.

"Well, with a twist. It was all about him. If great producers were leaving early, he wondered if he could engage them more. If lesser producers were, he thought about whether he could engage them at all."

"Sounds like a thoughtful guy. . . . Look, there's nothing wrong with the people on my team, if that's what you're suggesting; they're all engaged, great producers."

"I'm not talking about them."

Like many longtime tech managers Camila had known, Nolan was technically proficient, but his team was involved in so many different projects that he was challenged to keep up; they were doing work he never saw or perhaps didn't understand. He might have been their manager, but did he know how to help them? Or himself?

"How do you coach people with different experience than your own? Your remote employees?" Camila asked him. "How's that going? Or what do you do when 'how's it going?' isn't enough?"

Nolan took a long swallow of his soda to buy time to think. He wasn't sure. He had to admit: He hadn't been asked such a question in a very long time.

TAKE 1

Commentary by Christopher D. Adams

Christopher D. Adams is a performance consultant and instructional designer with more than 20 years of experience helping clients engage people, apply processes, and implement technology to improve human and organizational performance.

It's encouraging in this case that Camila and Nolan have the opportunity to work together. Creating a partnership between business and HR is a stated goal of Auruco's new CEO and a critical enabler of improved performance. But, what is the goal and focus of that partnership? Is it to bring Nolan back in line with HR procedures, or to improve the results of his team?

This case mentions several solutions or tactics that have been or could be put into place with Nolan and his team, including forced distribution performance rankings, individual goal setting, coaching, and reassignment. But these are all means. There is, conversely, very little discussion of the ends or results the organization needs to achieve through the implementation of these solutions.

For example, when Nolan was asked to implement forced distribution in performance reviews, he wasn't given a clear picture of how that would benefit the business. If the need was, as Nolan assumed, to control costs, then additional solutions other than eliminating employees with the lowest rankings might have been possible for such a small team. In the absence of clear goals and expectations, it was reasonable for Nolan to push back against using such a solution.

Before implementing anything, Camila and Nolan need to work in partnership to accomplish four things:

1. Clarify business goals for Auruco and related performance goals for Nolan's team.
2. Identify gaps between the desired and actual results as compared with those goals.
3. Uncover root causes for those gaps in business and performance results.
4. Select an appropriate set of solutions that align with root causes.

We can see a real impact of Nolan's team's performance on the business late in the case: The product line his team is developing is stalled. Here, the performance of Nolan's team is related to Auruco's goals. The case doesn't give clear metrics, but a stalled product affects budget, expense, time to market, and ultimately profit and revenue goals. Certainly, this should be of concern for Nolan. I would encourage Camila to offer to partner with Nolan to address this gap in business results because it will benefit Auruco as a whole, deepen their working partnership, and perhaps provide Nolan some needed insight on his team's performance. There is clearly a disconnect between Nolan's perceptions regarding his people's performance (he views them all as high producers) and the results they're currently achieving. Camila can help him greatly by working with him to identify the root causes for this gap.

There is a clear disconnect between Nolan's perception of his team and their actual performance.

One factor that is not clear from the case is the extent to which Nolan owns the responsibility for developing this product line. Is Nolan's team the only one working on the initiative? Does it include other developers across the organization? Does Nolan work across the organization with peers who also contribute resources? If Nolan is not the true owner, Camila may need to work with him to approach the business leader who holds ultimate responsibility for the business line. Again, this will give Camila and Nolan the opportunity to partner together and increase their access and credibility with leadership at Auruco.

Let's say Nolan is not the ultimate owner of the business need. Collaborating with the leader responsible for the product line could have several benefits. First, if other teams are working on the product line, Camila may be able to gather data that compare their performance with that of Nolan's team. If similar teams are meeting their productivity goals on the project, Camila may be able to identify specific behaviors that set this team apart. These data would enable Nolan to develop similar behaviors in his team members. And, it may help him better calibrate his perceptions of his team members' performance.

It may also uncover factors that are negatively affecting the performance of developers across many teams on the project (such as unclear or rapidly changing requirements). Although Nolan may lack the authority to address such issues directly, he and Camila could partner to influence leaders in Auruco to improve performance in this area.

Finally, working in partnership with the leader responsible for the product line may create an opportunity for that leader to observe and coach Nolan in the context of improving his team's work. As Nolan learns more about his leadership's business goals, his own management behaviors will gain greater, more meaningful context.

As Camila partners with Nolan to discover the factors contributing to the delayed product line, she should be mindful that such gaps in business results very seldom have just one cause. According to the case study, she's already thinking of solutions for Nolan and his team, such as coaching or reassignment. Camila is eager to help Nolan and no doubt has great experience providing a whole range of solutions. But, because gaps in business results are multicausal, multiple solutions are often required; Camila may not be able to provide all the necessary solutions. Her greatest value to Nolan and Auruco lies in asking the right questions, rather than simply putting yet another solution in place without a clear understanding of gaps and root causes.

This is a complex case, and I don't have enough data to recommend quick solutions. As I've described, I don't think Camila or Nolan have sufficient data either. But, they have a great opportunity to build a partnership that benefits Auruco by clearly defining the desired ends before selecting the means by which those ends might be achieved. As a tool, I'd recommend to Camila (and any HR professionals in her position) the book *Performance Consulting*, 3rd edition (Robinson et al. 2015), which provides a model, process, and techniques that align with my suggestions. In particular, the book's Gaps Map tool provides a way to visually describe gaps in business and performance results, root causes for those gaps, and solutions appropriate for addressing the causes.

TAKE 2

Commentary by Sharlyn Lauby

Sharlyn Lauby is president of ITM Group and author of the blog HR Bartender.

I view this as a performance management issue on several fronts: First, there's inconsistency. Nolan's team doesn't follow the same performance management process as everyone else. Second, individual attention is decreasing. Nolan's team isn't setting goals and doesn't have regular one-on-one meetings to discuss performance. Finally, investments aren't being made to help managers succeed. Camila senses that Nolan is overwhelmed and not able to keep up with his team.

Today, there are companies advertising that "if you come to work for us, we won't subject you to the dreadful annual performance review." Performance management is so much more than performance reviews, but this perception has become an obstacle that, as shown in this case study, must be dealt with.

To fully address this problem, I would also like to know:

- What kinds of training and development do managers at Auruco receive? Do managers receive training on how to conduct one-on-one meetings and performance reviews?
- How did Auruco introduce the forced distribution method? Why was this method chosen? Were managers given the opportunity to buy into the concept, and has it been effective?
- What's the current performance of Nolan's team? Are his methods effective? Is his team's performance suffering?

- Do any other managers share Nolan's concerns? Is this situation unique to him and his department, or do others feel the same?
- The new CEO wants more of a talent acquisition and development focus, which implies that there isn't one now. What's going on? And does Camila have the authority to do anything?

While it's possible that we'll never have all this information, the more understanding we can get, the easier it would be to proceed.

For Camila to be an effective coach, she must build trust and credibility. Based on this scenario, one might assume that Nolan won't be agreeable to "coaching" per se, but if Camila can come across as a trusted adviser, he might respond to her suggestions. I'd suggest one-on-one meetings where they can clear the air; the lunch meeting seems like a good start. While the forced distribution policy is no longer in place, Nolan's mistrust of HR still exists, and in his mind, Camila is part of HR. If Camila has some understanding of what happened with the policy, she might be able to convince Nolan that it won't happen again under her watch.

Camila is also going to have to figure out what the company goals are, and which ones are worth going to battle over. What are Auruco's vision, mission, and values? Does the company believe and live them? Think of this as a gap analysis—where is the company now, and where does it want to be? Camila can bring that same analysis to the HR department.

I would suggest to Camila that she find out her boundaries and her supporters. What can she do and how much authority does she have? If she was handpicked by the CEO, what boundaries have been established for her? Were employees informed of these boundaries when she started? She has to prove that she's qualified and earn people's respect. The same is true for Nolan. It's OK to express concerns about a company policy, but he must know that inconsistency can breed employee dissatisfaction, turnover, and lawsuits.

For its part, Auruco needs to establish performance standards, develop methods to evaluate performance, and then communicate those expectations. Part of this is figuring out what it's going to do about its "rock star" policy. Some companies are OK when very talented people don't follow the rules, but others aren't. The answer to that question says a lot about company culture and the way decisions are made. Either way, Auruco needs to make its position known. Employees are watching. If the company decides to condone this behavior, it opens the door to more of it.

Some of Auruco's problems are management issues that should be addressed in its development programs, provided the company has them. New managers should be onboarded and given the tools to do things like:

- Provide feedback to employees and senior leadership.
- Build consensus and collaboration.
- Conduct one-on-one meetings with employees.
- Evaluate performance.
- Practice self-awareness and self-management.

What is the company going to do about its "rock star" policy?

But if managers aren't receiving effective training, how do you get the organization to recognize that? This is where Camila has an advantage. As someone new to the organization, she has fresh eyes. She can use them to identify where training programs are nonexistent or need to be strengthened.

5

NO ROOM AT THE TOP

Cast of Characters at Open Wide Media

Jack Forsythe—Company Head

Betsy Forsythe—Company Head and Jack's Daughter

Dan Torres—Editor-in-Chief

Vicki Weber—Managing Editor

Rebecca Owen—Senior Editor

Claire Quinn—Associate Editor

Jess Perkins—Assistant Editor

The proposed raise was generous; who could say otherwise? Company heads Jack and Betsy Forsythe were fond of Claire and had told Dan Torres, the editor-in-chief, to go ahead and give her the bump in pay, but to be discreet about it. The last thing they wanted was the rest of the staff hearing about a 30 percent raise.

* * *

Claire Quinn was an associate editor with Open Wide Media Group. She was just over five years out of school and a reliable, creative, smart employee well regarded by her company. Recently, though, she had become frustrated. Her starting salary had grown incrementally each year, and now she was seeing younger friends—recent graduates—offered what she was currently earning, as well as some close college friends who'd gone to business school now entering a more lucrative job market. She had begun looking for other publishing jobs and, finding nothing in the area as interesting as the long-form feature writing she occasionally got assigned at her magazine job, she'd started to consider whether she should look for positions outside journalism or go to graduate or professional school herself.

Claire had arrived at Open Wide Media as an unpaid college intern for the company's flagship print publication, *City Eyes*. Interns had long been a key part of the company's successful business model. Once Claire graduated from college, she became a preferred candidate, first in line for a newly vacated editorial assistant position, a job she held for a little over a year before being promoted first to assistant editor and then last year to associate editor.

While her role expanded over the years to include more responsibilities and creative assignments, Claire continued to carry many of the duties of her first job—an accretion of tasks over the years and a seeming loss of none. It was a testament to her goodwill, energy, participation, and humor that she managed them. Other staff came to rely on her for efforts that her continuity and institutional knowledge made more efficient: seamlessly anticipating and arranging meetings, putting together actionable agendas, scheduling regular author calls, giving gentle reminders. In short, she did many things a managing editor would be expected to do—but without a managing editor's title or pay.

To friends who asked, Claire was quick to respond that her discontent wasn't only about money; she felt locked into a prescribed hierarchy that gave her little room to grow. She wanted to be part of a creative team, working to develop magazine stories and issues together under deadline, but long days were becoming routine with no end in sight, leaving her little room for reflective work. Performing, and excelling at, routine editorial tasks—proofreading, filing, copy editing, and scheduling—had made Claire a capable associate editor for the company's print and digital offerings, but she wasn't becoming any more skilled at developing a good story, which was what she loved to do.

Claire's job had become a mixture of intern, assistant, and associate editor responsibilities, but "wearing many hats" was wearing thin. The variety of things she was responsible for, Claire believed, kept her from fully participating in meetings or doing her best writing. At her current rate of development, she didn't see how she could achieve the autonomy, skill, and relatedness on the job that she had read were keys to career advancement. Claire had pored over the requisite career books about passion and doing what you love, as well as their opposites, such as *So Good They Can't Ignore You: Why Skills Trump Passion in the Quest for Work You Love* and *Quarterlife Crisis: The Unique Challenges of Life in Your Twenties*. That was Claire's quandary: develop skill or passion?

Claire had heard about other twentysomethings in the workplace who loved their jobs in today's journalism but couldn't rise into the rarer air of editorial management. She knew the almost-too-good-to-be-true story of the pair who quit traditional television news producer jobs to create their own targeted email newsletter. It may have had a start-up business model, but it succeeded as a flatter, more collaborative enterprise than what Claire experienced in the world of work.

Lately it seemed that all Claire's pitching in was simply hiding the fact that the company was understaffed, routinely crashing against deadlines, and barely bridging the seasonal gap between intern shifts. She scheduled staff meetings, distributed agendas and notes, handled freelance queries, edited features and departments, proofread, handled permissions, liaised with other magazine staff, and handled intern applications and interviews. Consequently, she was treated as favored personal assistant by the executive editors Jack and Betsy, who relied on her.

It frustrated Claire that her proposal to rotate office chores wasn't going to be implemented without Dan's direction. She also wondered why they were switching vendors so often; did this decision come from her bosses or higher up? The changing environment was a challenge for a staff like theirs to manage, and it all left little time for original work.

Open Wide Media

Open Wide Media is a family-owned company producing several regional print and digital publications and special events. For nearly 40 years, it has been owned by the Forsythe family, and day-to-day business is handled by the family head, Jack, and his eldest daughter, Betsy.

The company, which has an annual revenue of $2.5 million, publishes *City Eyes*—a city-centered lifestyle monthly—as well as four quarterlies with a variety of special-interest themes. A creative staff of 10 produces the print publications and digital platforms, and takes the lead on company-run special events. Circulation hovers around 20,000 monthly; print advertising revenue has thinned as digital and mobile markets have grown.

Magazine staff includes Editor-in-Chief Dan, Managing Editor Vicki Weber, and Senior Editor Rebecca Owen, all of whom have been with Open Wide Media for more than 15 years. The assistant editor, Jess Perkins, was hired last year from the intern pool. A large crop of unpaid interns circulate through the office on half-yearly assignments in editorial, design, and photography, and the publications couldn't go to press without them. Although the magazine has seen periodic turnovers at the entry level and lower-paying staff positions, there has been no room at the top for well over a decade.

In the Dark

Dan knew there was little financial transparency at Open Wide Media. He wasn't thrilled about how the intern group had grown over the years, and how they had become so necessary to the everyday function of the creative department, particularly. His budget was a moving target, and with advertising revenue falling off, he had to devise ways to keep the Forsythes happy and the staff engaged. Yet he was proud of the fact that even though growth was so flat, during his tenure things were stable, and he hadn't had to lay off staff.

Dan also knew he needed to create new revenue streams for the magazine business—and a series of custom publishing projects with the business team seemed like just the ticket. He hadn't presented his ideas to the Forsythes yet because he first wanted to talk to Vicki about the editorial staff's current workload, and how best to incorporate a couple new, short publishing schedules over the next few months. He hoped they would be short, anyway.

Claire's Proposal

At her latest performance and salary review, Claire had put forth something new—that the company create a position of features editor, which she would fill. It would enable the company to both schedule and budget features for the long term, and consequently better coordinate advertising. Such a master schedule was something magazine staff had long talked of, but a plan had eluded them. Claire explained how her current role would mesh with the new one, allowing her to circulate among the company's main print offerings, overseeing feature content and quality for each. Supported with staff input, she would synthesize and research feature ideas, commission freelance work, and oversee the writing of staff and freelancers, as well as edit and rewrite. Those tasks that didn't fit the new role could be renegotiated or reassigned to the current assistant editor, Jess. It all made perfect sense to Claire. She was trying to develop her purpose and mission, and get feedback.

When the senior staff was alone after Claire's review, Vicki said, "You know how I feel about Claire, but is it possible she expects too much from us?"

"Can we afford to add senior staff?" Rebecca added. "Is she asking for more responsibility than she can handle?"

Dan, who still hadn't shared the custom publishing project idea, wondered if Claire would accept the Forsythes' raise if they didn't agree to her new role.

Had Claire outgrown her job and organization, like others of her age and experience? Had the organization declined to grow and make room for her?

TAKE 1

Commentary by Tom Kaiden

Tom Kaiden is the chief operating officer of Visit Alexandria, in Alexandria, Virginia.

I particularly like this case because it reflects a common situation today: external disruption exacerbating internal tension. Open Wide Media is facing environmental pressure because of the economic disruption in the publishing industry. Yet all the internal players, from ownership down to interns, are trying to play by the old set of rules. And the longer they try, the more intractable the problem will get.

The publishing industry was extremely profitable before the digital age, but the major revenue source from that model—print advertising—is drying up. Certainly some online ad revenue has emerged, but not nearly as much as has been lost. Yet, Open Wide Media continues to operate much as it always has. Currently the company breaks down into seven levels of management:

1. Jack and Betsy (company heads)
2. Dan (editor-in-chief)
3. Vicki (managing editor)
4. Rebecca (senior editor)
5. Claire (associate editor)
6. Jess (assistant editor)
7. Interns (content and creative production)

A $2.5 million organization in a disrupted industry cannot be this top heavy. So, let's look at the case from the individual perspectives of several players.

Jack and Betsy

Jack and Betsy recognize Claire's talent, and are about to offer her a 30 percent raise, but they want to keep the raise quiet. To me, this brings up red flags everywhere. First, there is little evidence that the raise will address Claire's fundamental problem. Although she is frustrated by money, the bulk of her issues are caused by working long hours just to maintain the current project load, with no capacity for growth. A raise is likely to make her feel good for one or two pay cycles, but it will not address her bigger need for personal development.

The idea that salaries can be kept quiet is also unrealistic—this information almost always gets out. Employees talk to one another. Payroll reports are left on someone's desk. Salary information may be confidential, but executives should always be prepared for a leak. If the emergence of that information would be disruptive, then it's probably a bad idea.

The larger issue for Jack and Betsy, as owners, is to address the company's business model. They are holding tightly onto financial information, withholding it even from their editor-in-chief, Dan. They need Dan's help in identifying new profit streams, and in dispassionately identifying which elements of their current business are no longer profitable. There is no way to make room for the new without jettisoning some of the old.

Dan

As editor-in-chief, Dan is trying to juggle staff morale and owner expectations. It's an impossible task, unless he is willing to change the current business model. He also wants to introduce more work into the equation by bringing in the custom publishing projects. Dan needs to do something to free up resources to test this new idea, before officially rolling it out. But, he also shouldn't assume that custom publishing is the only new revenue prospect.

Dan's proud that there have been no layoffs, but zero turnover in management is not necessarily good for corporate culture. The absence of turnover has led to the current top-heavy structure that has many layers of editors, with much of the actual content and creative work being done by a revolving cast of unpaid interns. Dan needs to eval-

Zero turnover is not always good for corporate culture.

uate who on the team is generating the highest value for the company, and who is dynamic enough to adapt to a changing mix of work products. Modest turnover can actually be healthy for organizations and team members.

Claire

Claire is a smart, productive member of the team. But some of her discontent is misplaced and her expectations unrealistic. Her idea to create a new position for features editor may be what she wants personally, but if it doesn't generate value for the company, Open Wide Media shouldn't do it. It is not the company's job to make her happy; it's the company's job to meet the needs of the marketplace.

Claire may be part of the solution, however, if she can shift her focus away from herself and toward the organization's gaps. If Dan can engage her as he begins to develop new profit streams, she can take on some new challenges, grow her career, and generate income for the organization, which will also help support a salary increase and promotion.

* * *

A lot depends on senior management's ability to make strategic choices about eliminating programs and people that are no longer contributing to the company's viability, and to create a testing approach to develop new revenue streams. If those changes don't happen, then Claire should probably leave Open Wide Media and seek opportunities elsewhere. As noted earlier, turnover is not necessarily a bad thing. The pace of change in today's economy means that it's normal for employees to make changes and adaptations throughout their careers. Flexibility and learning are the hallmarks of career success.

Only considering our own needs is naive, but it will always be important to consider our skills and passions in the context of market needs. The sweet spot is where personal values, organizational values, and economic values intersect.

TAKE 2

Commentary by Vivian Blade

Vivian Blade is a talent management strategist, author, keynote speaker, leadership development trainer, and executive coach.

One of the biggest challenges facing Open Wide Media is the changing environment it operates in. The workplace now holds four generations with varying values and expectations. And the publishing industry is also different—readership has grown significantly in the digital and mobile platforms. However, Open Wide Media has been slow to transition in both of those areas. What are the implications? If the company is not innovative with its products, especially in the digital and mobile space, it will stagnate and lose market share and revenue. If it doesn't innovate its workplace, the company will fail to attract and retain the talent it needs to remain competitive.

The organization's structure—a small number of employees, temporary entry-level roles, and long-tenured senior-level employees—does not provide opportunities for personal growth and development.

Open Wide Media's leaders don't realize that pay is not the only motivator. They probably don't realize that employees like Claire can be motivated by factors such as meaningful work, early advancement, and work–life balance. They also must understand that employee retention is not one size fits all. They can research generational differences in the workplace using the many books and online resources available on the topic. Resources such as the "Table of Diversity" will help them explore the many dimensions of what makes people who they are (Miles-McDonald 2017). They also should talk with employees to find out what's important to them and to understand their career aspirations. With these insights, the senior team will be more equipped to understand how these influences apply to their business, and what actions they should take in response.

This disconnect is, in part, why Claire is so frustrated. Although Dan and Vicki have given Claire a lot of responsibility, allowing her to gain administrative experience she may not have gotten in a larger company, she feels stuck and undervalued. Vicki has allowed scope creep to occur with Claire's job responsibilities; she did not intentionally design Claire's role, periodically re-evaluate her workload, or even compensate her accordingly. She isn't fully utilizing the skills and talents that Claire possesses. Management is missing this opportunity to take someone who is committed to the company, and invest in her further development. If they do nothing, they will lose her.

The question management should be asking is, "Can we afford to lose Claire?" Consider the cost of turnover if Claire leaves. Will the offer to increase her salary be enough? Can they afford not to consider her proposal and promote her? They are already willing to increase her pay, so what is the risk otherwise? What are the benefits if her idea works?

> **Don't miss the opportunity to take someone who's committed to the company and invest in her development.**

Claire was smart to develop an idea for her next role. She realized that she couldn't wait around for someone else to manage her career. But, she should be prepared to support her recommendation with information on how the industry changes influence the need for the organization to change. She must also be able to demonstrate how this new role can work, given the constraints of the organization. Although Claire may think her proposal is well thought through, she should be somewhat flexible, taking into account the overall business needs and timing required to make changes.

In the meantime, she should continue looking for other opportunities outside the company. She should research salaries, using resources such as Salary.com, PayScale.com, or Glassdoor.com, to obtain data around what she should expect to be offered given the role, her skills, and her experience.

Claire may be forced to make some tough decisions about whether to stay or leave Open Wide Media. She should create a career plan now that will help her in the decision process later. How does this new role help her advance? How does it fit into her long-term career plan? What experience will she gain and how will it help her advance to the next level?

Like Claire, Open Wide Media should develop a long-term strategy. With the way the organization is structured—depending heavily on interns for production, and a focus on meeting current deadlines rather than projecting out to future issues—staff don't have the capacity to think strategically about what's next. The lack of a strategic plan, and the staff to focus on it, is a huge risk for Open Wide Media. Staff will miss the trends evolving around them and steadily fall behind.

Dan realizes that flat growth and unpredictable revenue have created volatility in the budget, making it tough to manage. But his ideas for the custom publishing projects are just short-term revenue solutions. They don't address what is needed for long-term, sustainable growth. And the organization's leaders aren't taking the time to figure this out.

Dan, Vicki, Rebecca, Jack, and Betsy must seriously consider the changes in the industry and revenue sources. They need to develop a strategic plan to ensure they stay competitive in the long run. Most immediately, Dan has to come up with some new, long-term ideas to bring in more revenue. Perhaps he is overwhelmed and has difficulty seeing beyond his own proposal, and feels threatened by the change suggested by Claire, who is committed and passionate enough to propose an option that could help the company and herself to grow. Is there an opportunity for both ideas to work?

Opportunities are ripe for both Open Wide Media and Claire. The decisions each make and the mindset with which they pull these opportunities together will result in either short-term, unsustainable bandages or long-term growth.

6

SPREAD THIN IN THE MIDDLE-MANAGEMENT SANDWICH

Cast of Characters at Bayside Group

Laura Mitchell—Marketing Director

Marshall Owen—Executive Director

Will Downs—Communications Staff Writer

Julie Kim—Digital Marketing Specialist

Walter Cleaver—Head of Board of Directors

Laura Mitchell was tired of putting out her executive director's fires. The maddening part was that they were all with staff. To the outside world, Marshall Owen, recently hired executive director of the Bayside Group, was a welcome addition to this venerable southern riverside town—a cosmopolitan outsider from the big city. But now

Will Downs, a fine writer with a nimble use of language, was irate and calling Laura at all hours, this time even managing to beat her alarm, and Will was not known for being an early riser.

"Just calm down, Will, and tell me exactly what he said."

"Well, first—I'm already backed up with his edits to the marketing plan, which I thought we needed to float by some board members this week, and then he wants prepared remarks for a meeting with the mayor, and now he's planning to speak to the Rotary this week and wants a 30-minute PowerPoint on the mixed-use project for the old shopping mall site."

"But that project doesn't exist!"

"It does now. He sketched it out already this morning, scanned it, and emailed it to me."

"That's insane. I mean . . . let me think. . . . OK. I've got a really nice program on the archaeology of the city market site. I gave it to the school board last year before Marshall arrived. Give him that instead."

"And I explain this how?"

"I'll talk to Marshall." Laura wondered if her boss even knew what the Rotary was.

Out With the Rose Queen

The Bayside Group is a nonprofit economic development group, with a public-private partnership, advocating for city business development. It has an independent board of directors who set the mission and approve all major decisions, including staffing. Founded in the early 1990s after a period of recession and slow economic growth, the Group has become an integral part of the city's organizational structure, supporting its overall mission and business goals.

But over the past few years, the board had clashed with Mary Rose, Marshall's predecessor. Walter Cleaver, chairman of the board, had been relieved when she'd finally stepped down last year, faced with what amounted to a no-confidence vote from the board.

Walter knew that the staff liked and admired Mary Rose. She was one of the oldest members of one of the oldest families in the city, and affectionately dubbed the Rose Queen. She'd fought for the first community garden space, practically engineered its city-sponsored compost deliveries, and still grew the garden's best tomatoes. She was a city institution, but she had also become a lightning rod for Walter's development plan—even supporting a second hearing on the issue despite Walter's belief that opposition had died down.

It was a time of transition for the Bayside Group, Walter reasoned, and Mary Rose, who in past decades had tirelessly and almost single-handedly saved historic residential blocks from the wrecking ball, was out of step with the city's new economic landscape. He thought that she was too quick to give voice to longtime residents who were anxious about their taxes and resistant to change, instead of trying to guide them toward a new economic vision for the city.

Walter's vision, simply put, was that the Group had to find ways to invigorate the city's tax base. The local businesses lining the historic main street were feeling pressure from online retailers, and the city budget, still recovering from a hurricane of historic proportions several years ago, had no room for badly needed school infrastructure improvements. But tourism was booming at nearby resorts and beaches, and a new culinary school in an old refurbished high school building was planning to bring a celebrity chef to town. Walter was hopeful the Bayside Group could exploit their proximity to such attractions.

Friends since graduate school, Walter had great faith in Marshall's ability to execute his vision. Marshall had spent his career in the museum world, where he'd risen in the curatorial ranks to become director of one of the country's most prestigious museums. Walter saw his friend as having the management, business, and artistic sensibilities that Mary Rose lacked; qualities that would benefit the Bayside Group. He had planted the seed with Marshall long ago, but only recently saw it bear fruit when, during a dinner in the city, Marshall's interest seemed piqued. He'd told Walter he was tired of exhibition cost overruns, willful curators, and board intransigence, and he was ready for a new opportunity.

"Make Some Artistic Enhancements"

What Marshall should be doing, Laura muttered to herself, was reviewing the marketing campaign so it would be ready to launch at next month's board meeting. She had delivered it to him last week, but had received not so much as an email acknowledgment. At their weekly staff meeting, he had referred obliquely to "making some artistic enhancements," but she had no idea what he meant—changes to the look of the plan or the plan itself? He also had a way of shutting down discussion, even in a meeting, that she found unnerving.

"He means that he wants to include more community artists," sighed Julie Kim, the digital specialist. It was late. Everyone else had gone home. Julie stood in the doorway, on her way home herself. "He doesn't think we've included enough artistic voices in the past, and that's what the bigger cities do. They successfully accentuate their artistic appeal."

Laura turned to Julie, surprised but interested. "You read my mind. How do you know this?"

"Marshall told me, when we had drinks last night," Julie said. "Look, don't hate me, but this place has gotten so weird, I just have to look out for myself."

Laura took a deep breath. "I'm sorry you feel that way. It has been different, I agree. But Marshall shouldn't share work ideas with you out of the office like that. Especially when we're not all present."

"I don't know, you could have come, we asked you."

Laura realized that as digital marketing specialist, Julie was the focus of much of Marshall's attention. He seemed to request changes to the website almost daily, whether it was because of an exhibition he'd just attended, a newspaper article he'd read recently, or someone he'd spoken to at dinner the night before. But it was too late to make significant changes to the marketing campaign and expect her to find a way to incorporate them. She'd have to conduct interviews with local artists, and those she couldn't include would be offended. It would be slapdash.

"Maybe next time," Laura responded.

"A Group Effort"

The following afternoon, Marshall poked his head into Laura's office. "Thanks for sending the revisions last night. I like your idea about featuring the Impressionists exhibition in the marketing piece—it creates kind of an artistic framework for the whole look. Not many people know about that sculpture garden in the old fairgrounds."

"Well, I think it was your idea, but thanks, I like it, too." Laura wondered if what she said was actually true: Did she like the revisions she had stayed up most of the night to make, or was it simply an attempt to placate her boss?

"No, we all worked together to make that happen," Marshall said magnanimously. "A group effort, don't be modest."

Laura looked at Marshall and tried to smile. "Do you have time for lunch this week?"

"How about tomorrow, before I leave for the Great Cities Conference?" he replied. "And Will said you wanted to talk to me. . . . By the way, I really need him to write me a speech. I'd like to take it with me—something to read on the flight."

"What about the Rotary?"

"Gosh, I almost forgot! It's tomorrow night! Can you do it in my place?"

"Sure. Not to worry," said Laura.

Out the Door?

The three days Marshall was away were chaotic. He called the office daily needing calendar reminders and research to share with conference participants. He claimed the website wasn't up-to-date and that the online calendar wasn't accurate, and insisted that Julie stop whatever she was doing to make immediate updates and confirm them with him. She began to complain to Laura about stress, that she felt micromanaged and mistrusted. Marshall also emailed the staff daily to report on conference sessions that he found relevant to their work, suggesting ideas for future projects and initiatives, and directing them to schedule meetings upon his return.

Will, who Laura noticed had been late with the week's press kit, was busy sending Marshall drafts of a 30-minute talk on the Group's recent innovations and successes for business investment. He promised Laura that the overdue press packet would be ready before the end of the week.

Nobody could do anything for the new marketing plan. Laura gave the same talk to the Rotary she'd given to the school board the year before.

Marshall returned to the office energized. "I'm not sure about the Impressionists now," he said. "I saw a Brancusi show that the city museum should get. Let's set up a meeting with the museum director about whether they could fit this in their schedule—a special event kind of thing—it would be amazing."

Later that day, Will resigned to join the speechwriting team of a politician with national aspirations; Julie, without a job offer in hand, gave her notice the following morning. Both were apologetic and conciliatory, yet emphatically advised Laura to follow them out the door.

Should she leave? Or could she find a way to persuade her boss to be more strategic? Any decision to replace departing staff would involve the board, but it would accomplish little if she couldn't deliver a marketing plan that everyone could get behind. The board might have feuded with Bayside Group's mission before, but what if now they unanimously accomplished nothing?

She took a deep breath and walked down the hall to Marshall's office.

"Hey, come on in," Marshall said, waving Laura in from behind his desk. "Walter Cleaver told me how much he learned at your Rotary talk the other night. He said it was a real eye-opener about our early history."

Laura smiled, pretty certain that Walter Cleaver had heard the same talk the year before.

TAKE 1

Commentary by Rick Rittmaster

Rick Rittmaster is the manager of learning and development at MTS, a global supplier of high-performance test systems and sensors.

I tend to think of these situations in two categories:
1. macro, systemic factors
2. micro, individual behaviors.

These factors operate within the same system.

From a systems perspective, Bayside Group is an organization in transition. Both Walter's perspective and the needs of the city indicate that its vision is changing. The problem stems from the fact that its vision is significantly out of focus and it is lacking leadership. It is unclear where this organization is going, and as a result there is no alignment around tasks, projects, and larger initiatives. This lack of clarity is limiting the organization's ability to advance the needs of the community it supports and is creating angst among its employees.

It's common for people and teams to hold different perceptions around what it means to be strategic. For some, like Laura, strategic thinking involves setting future targets, and then diligently working toward those goals. For others, like Marshall, strategic thinking means taking advantage of opportunities in the moment that didn't previously exist. Intuitively, it's clear that having both perspectives on a team is good. However, these different perceptions can also lead to negative tensions, as seen within the Bayside Group.

From an individual perspective, a significant theme at the Group is a lack of trust. You can see it in Marshall's micromanaging, Laura's lack of accountability, and the team's inability to have direct and challenging discussions. Additionally, there is ample research that middle managers are the most stressed, least happy individuals within an organization, all of which validates the tension and challenges that Laura is facing. Other common factors within this case study include a new leader failing to account for the organization's existing culture. But, as I have commonly found in real life, there is no one "right" or "wrong" person. Conflict of this nature is almost always a combination of good intentions and opportunities for better collaboration; I see this mix within Bayside Group.

Before sharing any recommendations, it is important to begin from a place of empathy. I would avoid providing any initial recommendations (insofar as they point to direct solutions) and instead ask questions that guide Laura, Bayside Group, and others toward a productive solution. These questions have the added benefit of testing my recommendations without risking buy-in around next steps.

Laura has a very important role at Bayside Group, but also appears to have conflicting motivations that are affecting her engagement. It isn't clear if or why Laura would want to stick with the organization.

From an individual perspective, a significant theme at Bayside is a lack of trust.

I would want to ask Laura questions that focus on her internal drivers and motivation. What are her beliefs about Bayside Group, both in terms of its past accomplishments and possibilities for the future? What does she want to get out of her experience at the organization? How realistic are her expectations? What does a "good" outcome look like from her point of view?

Bayside Group has traditionally been an integral part of the city's organizational structure, supporting its mission and goals. However, the current environment indicates that recent efforts are misaligned and out of date. I would ask the organization questions that primarily focus on its purpose moving forward. Simply put, what does Bayside Group do? Where does it add the most value? Do businesses and citizens place the same value in its services as when the Group was founded? Where is it failing to meet expectations for its customers and stakeholders? Bayside Group's management must first answer these questions and then secure the board's approval.

Marshall must address his lack of focus, overly hands-on approach, and failure to account for the existing culture of the organization. My questions for him would focus on bringing certain elements of his management style into clearer focus: How have you been successful in past roles? Do those same strategies apply in this situation? You are not a local, and the previous leader had deep roots in the community. How has this fact affected how you lead the organization? How will Bayside Group account for the recent departures in staff? Are there any lessons learned from the employees who are leaving the organization?

Any sustainable recommendations would have to include Walter's perspective because he was the impetus for much of the change. I would focus my questions for Walter on his views of the organization's future: What does the Bayside Group of the future look like? Is it currently on a path toward that future? What does effective leadership look like, in your opinion? What was the vetting process for hiring Marshall? How well do Marshall's actions demonstrate effective leadership?

Although this additional context would help me understand the beliefs and values in play and analyze root causes, it's still important to remember that working with people is rarely straightforward. Thus, the simplest solutions often provide the biggest impact.

With that in mind, clearer accountabilities and a more focused organizational vision are two initial recommendations that would certainly benefit Bayside Group. How these problems are addressed is incredibly important. Any initial approach needs to do two things: First, allow for individual perspectives to be heard, and second, address business or operational concerns.

A well-facilitated SWOT discussion (strengths, weaknesses, opportunities, threats) can often address both of these topics. Any SWOT discussion should quickly be followed with a concrete definition of the problem or problems that the team will address. And ideally, problem statements would include both internal and external improvements. Because the team is now just two people (Laura and Marshall), a lessons learned discussion could also provide an effective alternative to a SWOT analysis. Whether SWOT or lessons learned, they need to devote specific questions to addressing the opportunity for clearer accountability. Both of these facilitation tools would lend themselves to exploring these topics in a healthy manner. Lastly, a RACI chart (detailing who is responsible, accountable, consulted, or informed) could help document decisions made around accountabilities and updated roles and responsibilities. Any such steps would not necessarily involve the board, although that would be a decision for Laura and Marshall. The board, however, should be informed of the analysis's outcome.

This approach requires an expert to facilitate the discussion, but the facilitator must balance guiding the conversation without providing too much personal input. People in pain (and there is most certainly some element of pain within Bayside Group) need to be heard, and the facilitator must act as a conduit for that.

Beyond the initial solution, approaches around establishing team norms, process mapping, and even stakeholder-focused groups would all be highly beneficial. However, the application of these solutions should be driven by a clear and aligned understanding of the problems the team is trying to solve.

As for any tools or resources, I would suggest trying to balance the two perspectives I defined at the outset: a good understanding of the big, important problems and how a specific tool can help solve them, as well as the smaller, more achievable first steps—how the tool can help people make progress in an incremental but meaningful way. It's an important balance, because you must always have a line of sight to the ultimate goal, while still encouraging daily actions that lead to success.

Any tools should build toward a common view of the problem or problems. This may be as simple as doing a SWOT analysis, but other situations may require a more robust assessment. The People Capability Maturity Model (PCMM), for example, is a very thorough exercise targeting specific developmental needs for a team, department, or entire organization. It helps the organization understand the maturity of its current people practices, and provides a useful perspective around how to localize and guide the maturation of the practices that are most effective. With teamwork as a general theme, the PCMM can identify specific areas of opportunity for Bayside Group to focus on.

Additionally, and after some type of organizational assessment, I would recommend tools and resources focused on team collaboration issues. Patrick Lencioni's 2002 book, *The Five Dysfunctions of a Team,* has a nice resource for guiding a team through a series of activities and discussions to foster more trust and collaboration. Many tools of this nature exist; the critical benefit is providing a clear, pragmatic process to promote team engagement and alignment for everyone involved. Finally, regarding leadership: Taking on a new leadership role is extremely challenging. As the fantastic book *The First 90 Days: Proven Strategies for Getting Up to Speed Faster and Smarter* (Watkins 2013) articulates, one of the biggest risk factors is failing to adjust for the existing culture.

Unfortunately, I do believe the situation at Bayside Group is a common scenario. However, there are steps that can be taken to avoid these problems. At the simplest level, organizations break down when the foundations of teamwork are not in place. If individuals are unclear about their roles and responsibilities, if there is a lack of trust within the team, and if there is confusion around the purpose of the organization, then the team's ability to be successful will be greatly affected. While focusing on areas like roles and responsibilities is not the most exciting part of leadership work, it is extremely valuable. The mundane, almost boring nature of these foundational elements is why they tend to get overlooked. And not surprisingly, it's where problems also tend to start.

It is important to state that avoiding these problems does not require the title of president. Anyone in an organization can, and should, proactively seek to address concerns around the responsibilities and purpose of their role. Leaders are often grateful, if not relieved, to have a willing and collaborative participant on this topic.

TAKE 2

Commentary by Ben Locwin

Ben Locwin is CEO of a healthcare consulting organization. He has held executive roles for top pharmaceutical companies and developed human performance models for a variety of organizations.

The ultimate issue in this case study is "shiny object syndrome," where Marshall (and, frankly, the board) can't decide on a course of action and supportive strategy, so he chases after every single new idea that comes up. That is a course destined to founder. Specifically, with the team in charge of execution, Marshall is completely inept at crafting and executing a tangible strategy, which has led to uncertainty among the team, high attrition, and a frustrated senior member (Laura).

There's an interesting phenomenon that occurs when an outsider —in this case, Marshall—comes into a fairly insular group, and that is the halo effect. The outsider is often given undue admiration and attention because they aren't part of the social group. Their words are lavished with outsized importance because they came from "outside." But Marshall, at this level and point in his career, is unable to be rehabilitated. The principally value-added action would be to replace him forthwith. He clearly doesn't have a strategic vision or a plan of attack, hence his scattered coverage of items of varying importance. There's also an issue with scalability in his application of an approach—just because something works for a big-city event, for example, doesn't mean a smaller version of that will work in a town. It's entirely different thinking—not just shrinking the big vision to fit the small.

Choosing a true leader who has a vision compatible with what the town is interested in would lead to the highest probability of success, but Bayside Group's board of directors did not do that. The whole board, in all likelihood, needs to have their tenure challenged. The city's needs have changed since the early 1990s, so the whole overall perspective of Bayside Group needs to change, too.

Regarding Laura, I would suggest that she stay if she thinks she can continue to enjoy the work, or leave if she can't work well with Marshall. She shouldn't think that leaving is the best choice, because that brings its own risks. But she should also know that she will not be able to change how Marshall conceives of his plans or manages the Group and its resources. Most of these practices are entrenched and highly resistant to modification. This is why she needs to decide if she can live with, and function within, his management style—no amount of commentary she gives will appreciably change how he operates.

I'd recommend that Laura think about this situation from a psychological compatibility perspective. She doesn't need to let her inertia keep her there, if

> **The ultimate issue in this case study is "shiny object syndrome."**

she truly feels like too many pieces are broken and that Marshall can't be reformed. On the other hand, Will and Julie were also artifices of the past ways of working, which clearly aren't the direction Marshall and the executives want to move. It will be easier to make changes happen once they hire replacements for Will and Julie, based on their technical merits and ability to conform to the new perspectives.

As for Walter, who heads up the board of directors, sometimes getting rid of those who subscribe to the past's school of thought paves the way for more contemporary views. Not all former leaders are compatible with what the future will hold. However, Walter needs to be careful. He has no evidence that his own proposal to invigorate the tax base will work.

I would suggest everyone—Laura, Walter, Marshall, and the board members—read Kouzes and Posner's *The Leadership Challenge* (2012), which is a great book on the overall aspects of leadership from a variety of different perspectives and angles. It shows that while leadership doesn't look the same in every scenario, it is indeed about making the business a better place tomorrow than it was today. In this sense, particular elements such as trust, communication, and creating a vision are discussed in ways that make many of Marshall's and Bayside Group's deficiencies stand out starkly.

This is an exceedingly common scenario. I sit on several nonprofit and for-profit boards of directors, and I believe that determining who should be (or stay) in leadership is a primary concern and motivating force for improving the future. Not every installed leader or manager will work under every situation. So, understanding as best as possible the underlying perspectives, biases, and interpersonal traits each leader has in each role—and how those are related to potential success or failure within the organization given its particular challenges—is an absolutely critical element.

For example, Steve Jobs is well-known for having turned Apple around in stellar fashion. For that organization at that time and in that market, he was absolutely the right leader and a visionary. But if you had put him instead at the helm of Yahoo! when Marissa Mayer took over, he would have failed spectacularly. The two initial conditions were not the same, and therefore the outcomes would have been dramatically different. It's important for readers to note, as well, that even analyzing Steve Jobs and Marissa Mayer in these contexts is post hoc reasoning: Only by seeing what he did, can we say "he was the right person for that role." There's no good way of doing this in advance, and that's why it's always a business risk.

7

"IT COULDN'T HAPPEN HERE"

Cast of Characters

Monica Gannon—Bank Street Branch Manager

Robert and Betty Jones—Longtime Bank Street Branch Customers

Anthony Cobb—Bank Street Branch Assistant Manager

Charlie McDaniel—Prosperity Trust Bank Regional Manager

Dale Gannon—Monica's Building Contractor Husband

"How does that even happen?" Robert Jones put his hand to his face in seeming mock alarm, turning to his wife, Betty. But she didn't answer, just shook her head.

Sitting across from them, Monica Gannon knew that Robert's question was hardly rhetorical. The Joneses were her longtime customers, and Robert wanted assurance that the financial scandal all over the news that morning—one more retail bank faltering due to its own malfeasance—wouldn't happen here.

"I know it's unnerving to read such stories," said Monica. "But there are ethics standards that we adhere to; it couldn't happen here."

"I've read that it starts with the regional managers," Robert continued. "That they set goals for their branches and people throughout the day, sometimes four times a day!" He looked from his wife to Monica for confirmation.

"We don't have those kinds of quotas here. Honestly, I don't think anyone could last very long in such a place; it would be too stressful," said Monica, shaking her head and trying to sound reassuring. "It seems the opposite of what community banking should be, I know."

Betty took her husband's sleeve as she stood to leave. "We don't have to worry, Robert. Monica's looked after us for a long time."

"Since the Bank Street Branch opened in the nineties," said Robert.

"You know it's been my pleasure," said Monica, rising from behind her desk.

Prosperity Trust Bank

Prosperity Trust Bank (PTB) is the largest financial institution in its five-state region. It started out as a small regional bank more than a century ago, expanding in the 1970s to provide a full range of commercial and consumer banking, as well as wealth management offerings. Although PTB emphasizes its community banking beginnings, local leadership, and personalized service, today its some 2,500 employees serve a million customers at 200 branches. This community bank has assets of $15 billion.

Throughout the year, PTB recognizes top-performing branches, managers, and employees formally and informally. Consequently, intense competition has developed among branches for top talent, and it's becoming increasingly common for lower-performing branches to poach top talent from the higher performers.

The future of PTB's consumer banking division will be determined by how well it is able to respond to challenges from online competitors, who can more quickly handle simple transactional interactions, and other brick-and-mortar branches, which are working to distinguish their financial customer service brand. Adding to the competitive environment, the PTB board is pushing to expand through mergers and acquisitions, to avoid becoming an M&A target itself.

Trust and Diplomacy

It was late in the evening; the tellers were gone and the bank closed to customers. Anthony Cobb, the assistant manager at the Bank Street Branch, popped his head into Monica's office. Before he could speak, Monica began without looking up:

"Before you repost that position, Anthony, take a look at this edited job description. The kind of personality you want in that job—outgoing, yes, but add this: 'A high level of trust and diplomacy in addition to expected courtesy and tact.'"

Anthony smiled at his boss. "It's to be a personal banker, not an ambassador. Aren't you setting the bar a little high?"

"Aren't you the one who said candidates were asking for a script and a set of questions?"

"They came from call centers, they didn't know any better."

"My point exactly. Rewrite the job description," Monica said with a grin, tapping her computer keyboard. "There, just sent it to you."

"How did you ever hire me?" Anthony asked, laughing, backing out the door.

"Hey, remember, I'm out all day tomorrow with the developers and architects at the college site," Monica said. "Can you handle the Spring Street conference call without going crazy? I know they're understaffed, but—"

"About that," Anthony interrupted her, then stopped to take a breath before continuing.

But Monica cut him off. "Don't say it!" she said as she threw up her arms in alarm. "They offered you the manager's job, didn't they?"

"It's a good job," said Anthony. "And I think I can really make a difference there."

"I'm talking to Charlie—that's not right," Monica said, immediately beginning an email to the regional manager. "And I mean not for you or for me or this bank."

"Please don't be so dramatic," Anthony said. "I owe this place so much, you know that. I've learned everything from you."

Musical Chairs: A History

Monica was the first assistant manager of PTB's suburban Bank Street Branch when it opened in 1994 with 20 employees. A decade later, the Spring Street Branch opened in a renovated part of downtown, and four Bank Street employees were reassigned there, including Monica's boss. She was then promoted to Bank Street Branch manager. Unfortunately, Spring Street has not performed as well as PTB's parent company had hoped—many of its urban retail neighbors, challenged by online competition, have disappeared, reducing foot traffic. Last year, when Spring Street's manager left to join a competitor across town, Monica was offered the job. But she declined, in spite of a nice salary increase, because her daughter's high school was five minutes away from the Bank Street location.

Besides, Monica had long considered the Spring Street Branch a thorn in her side. Her regional manager, Charlie, often scheduled her in conference calls and face-to-face meetings with Spring Street personnel in an effort to understand and compare the data behind her success and the other bank's difficulties. As a result, her own branch's productivity was slipping. As Monica saw it, her staff was often pulled away by a competitor bank's requests, rather than those from bank customers.

Sometimes Monica wondered if her branch and Spring Street could find a way to truly collaborate. Was that possible?

"Not So Fast"

"Hey, I hear congratulations are in order," said Charlie, who had asked Monica to meet him before their usual monthly lunch. "Bank Street is still number one—lunch on me."

Monica eyed him warily. "You know, it's hard to stay on top if I keep losing people, but thanks."

"You mean Anthony? It's a good move for him. Don't you think he's ready?"

"Probably, but I really rely on him. He's been doing all our hiring and training for the past year. He knows the product lines better than anybody. Everybody relies on him, not just me."

"Maybe you rely on him too much."

"So, let me give him a raise and a new title."

"You're just putting off the inevitable."

"Hey, not so fast. I trained that kid out of high school."

"Gotta let go sometime."

The Human Element

Back when Monica was named branch manager, her husband, Dale, had stopped by the bank. He was a building contractor, and she valued his opinion about office space and function.

"This reminds me of a train station, hon," he said as he looked around the cavernous marble lobby. "What's the main thing you want to do here? It seems like just move people."

Monica grew pensive; Dale smiled, "Let me suggest something else." With that, he grabbed the notepad on her desk and quickly transformed the lobby into several light-filled, glass-walled offices.

Monica had kept that sketch until, over time, it had become reality. The Bank Street Branch lobby now looked more like one of the high-end brokerage offices downtown. All the better to do the business she knew was the bank's future—clients opening new accounts and seeking advice for their complex wealth management problems, face-to-face, at the branch. The human element would become more focused on advice-giving and strategies, and less on transactional interactions. More and more, customers would begin to look at the bank and other financial enterprises as a partner in making sound financial decisions.

The question was: How many branches would thrive in that new order?

Could It Happen Here?

At lunch, Charlie had delivered the new quarterly regional plan for Bank Street Branch: add to its daily solutions goals and keep an eye on productivity numbers. But with Anthony leaving, Monica wasn't sure how that would happen. Although two new personal bankers were coming on, they were inexperienced with bank protocols. They needed more training, but there was no one and no time to do it. She could instruct all the tellers on their new goals—such as how many referrals they were required to make by next quarter—but she would need to find an assistant manager and more customer service reps to aggressively address these new goals. And, she worried that despite being out of the office most days on bank business, she would have to make up the rest somehow.

Charlie's advice? "Just fill the seats, and you'll make your numbers."

TAKE 1

Commentary by Joe Willmore

A leader in the field of human performance, Joe Willmore is a consultant for a range of organizations and the author of numerous publications on performance improvement.

Thomas Gilbert, one of the giants of performance improvement, talked about the "cult of knowledge," in which organizations treat knowledge as if it is an end in itself. But just because you have smart, knowledgeable people in your organization doesn't mean you get good performance, and that certainly applies in this case. Of course, I'd rather have an organization full of bright, talented, and highly skilled people than one of dumb, underskilled performers. But there is a tendency to assume that if only we had "good people" then we'd get good results. And that is not the case.

Prosperity Trust Bank is a great example of an organization that puts so much focus on talent, to the point where branches poach talent from one another. This organizational culture creates internal competition, lack of trust, and a tendency for managers to want to "hang on" to talented performers, even if it means denying chances for promotion or growth. Ultimately, this hurts the organization because it creates a culture of distrust where branches compete against one another. I've seen organizations where senior managers actually denied internal promotions or low-balled evaluations because they didn't want to draw attention to high-potential employees who they intended to keep for their business unit.

In this case, I'd want to talk to senior management at PTB and find out what their business goals are. I'd ask, "What does success look like?" Answers to that question would allow me (as a performance consultant) to identify the business priorities and what the branches need to focus on. While the case references "numbers" for the branches, we don't know how they fit into business priorities. Always start by identifying "job one," or what the strategic imperatives are for the organization. Once you've done that, you'll know if what you're focusing on is a contributor to that priority or just a distraction.

Right now, it's easy for branch managers to get distracted at PTB. This case brings up a range of issues, but it's not clear (because we don't know the strategic priorities) if those issues are relevant or tangential to the business goals.

Just because you have smart, knowledgeable people doesn't mean you get good performance.

Absent that direction from senior management, the performance issue I'd focus on is how to improve the Spring Street Branch. Improving suboptimal performance (in an individual, a team, a work unit, or a business unit) is always challenging, but this is what performance improvement is about. And one of the fastest and easiest ways to improve performance is to look at an exemplar—in this case, Monica and the Bank Street Branch.

The idea is to look at the exemplar and determine what makes their performers so good. In many cases, the performers (or in this case, the manager—Monica) may not even know. But you can figure this out by identifying key performance results and doing a root cause analysis or influence analysis to determine what has the biggest impact on their performance and why they get better numbers than anyone else.

We're used to thinking of top performers (either individuals or business units) as being freaks of nature—born great or with attributes that make them unique. Sometimes that is the case. But in my experience, exemplars are usually better because they do the "blocking and tackling" better than other employees or functions. They may have removed unnecessary process steps. Or, conversely, they may have added steps to a key work process that result in better quality or happier customers. They may do a better job using information that everyone gets, like anticipating customer requests or individualizing service so customers feel special. Or maybe they created job aids that help minimize mistakes or improve service delivery. These actions or solutions could all be put in a box and given to other employees or units.

So, I'd start by identifying what makes the Bank Street Branch so successful. I'd start with Monica. I suspect she'd say, "the quality of the personnel," but I'd likely discount that. Why? For starters, remember Gilbert's cult of knowledge. But more specifically, Spring Street Branch has poached lots of talented people, and presumably other new managers were successful elsewhere—but the branch still underperforms. I'd need to dig deeper than just assume that if the Spring Street Branch gets better employees, all will be copacetic. But I'm confident that by doing a root cause analysis, I'd be able to identify what makes Bank Street Branch so successful, and identify some elements that I can transfer to other branches that are lagging.

TAKE 2

Commentary by Glen B. Earl

Glen B. Earl is the department chair of the Industrial/Organizational Psychology Program for The Chicago School of Professional Psychology, Dallas, Texas, campus.

There are two main problems in this case study. The first is the churn of employees, not only to competitors, but to different branches within the organization. High turnover speaks to low employee engagement, low morale, and poor customer service.

The second is the focus on completing tasks—that is, "hitting the numbers"—and little, if any, rewards for relationships, such as providing excellent customer service. This is a fast road to implosion. Organizations and their leaders are easily seduced by quickly rising profits, but downturn is inevitable if customers leave, taking their money with them, or leaders pillage their own company.

As we have seen in the news regarding the misdeeds of some well-known financial institutions, employees are sometimes given impossible, constantly changing goals, with little resources to achieve them and negative consequences if they're not met. Such a scenario never works; if it appears to, it is often because high-ranking internal personnel are forcing lower-level employees to break laws, act unethically, or go against their own company standards.

Robert and Betty Jones have every right to be concerned about their hard-earned money. When people's money is threatened, their sense of physical and emotional safety, security, and well-being are threatened. This is where empathetic and caring customer-service skills are paramount—branch employees are the frontline, customer-facing employees. A branch, in fact the whole bank, will rise or fall on its employees' customer-care skills.

There are many well-founded and successful approaches to properly address these issues. The first is creating a successful incumbent profile, and then developing a behavioral interviewing process. The end goal is for new hires and internal transfers to have a good job–person fit: fit with the role, fit with the bank's culture, and fit with the hiring manager.

After hiring for fit, the next step is proper training. The focus should be on task and relationship training. New employees need to understand the job and be able to accomplish the job task requirements; in this case, meeting production goals. But the training also needs to focus on relationships; that is, providing superior customer service.

My major recommendation for Monica would be to stay at the branch where she is right now; her family is vastly more important than her job. Being in high school is a very busy time, monumental in scope, activity, and preparation for the future. As a parent, being close, physically and emotionally, is critical for demonstrating support as your high school student is making many big life decisions.

For the organization, reviewing the culture and making some major changes is paramount. The current culture and business models are not sustainable; they will eventually collapse in on themselves, just as occurred in the Great Recession. An organization that continues to raid itself will eventually fall, and assuredly fail.

Anthony should take the promotion, but be mindful that much of his success is because of Monica's leadership style and her encouraging him to shine in his strengths, such as training and developing employees. He needs to be able to focus on the relationship side, as well as meet production goals as the new branch manager. I'd advise him to continue to use Monica as his mentor and guide. Once he becomes the branch manager, one of his first and most important tasks would be to find a person who is strong in relationships, provides excellent customer

An organization that continues to raid itself will eventually fall, and assuredly fail.

care, and is passionate about developing fellow employees.

Beyond interviews and traditional background checks, commercial pre-employment tests and personality assessments now exist that focus on honesty, dependability, job–person fit, sales, and customer service. You can try to assess a candidate's level of honesty, and whether a person is a good fit for the company culture, the job, and the hiring manager. For example, I'd want to know if a person is better suited to sales. And, I'd want to know who my people-focused employees are, so I can put them where they can best help the company with their heart and people skills. More and more, financial institutions can use a variety of tools to evaluate new employees' suitability for financial work, risk avoidance, and customer service. The memory of those banks that failed as a result of the recent recession is still fresh in a lot of minds.

Some years ago, I worked for a Fortune 100 financial services company. It had 60,000 employees, and 50 percent annual, voluntary turnover. How can a company survive when half of its employees are brand new every year? The company's motto was to "dominate the market," and at that point, it did. But shortly thereafter, the company failed. Thousands of employees were laid off, and its divisions were pulled apart and sold to other companies. In just a few short years, this company went from Fortune 100 status to nonexistent.

Prosperity Trust Bank could be on the road to a similar fate if it's not careful.

8

"WE'VE ALWAYS BEEN FINE"

Cast of Characters

Ben White—Manager of the Rest Easy Hotel

Shirley and Grant White, Ben's Aunt and Father—Former Managers (and Current Employees) of the Rest Easy Hotel

Jamie Barron—Performance Consultant, Amity Group

"History Just Means Old"

Ben had been avoiding the call from Atlanta all week. When the 678 area code appeared in his cell phone, he ignored it. Then it popped up on the hotel reservation desk, and he let the call go to voicemail. Finally, his aunt Shirley, seated across from him on the porch on a quiet Friday evening, picked up his ringing phone, answered it, and handed it to him, saying simply, "Phone for you, sweetie."

Ben glared at her, but took the call. The conversation was brief, cordial, and to the point: Jamie Barron, a performance consultant from corporate headquarters, was in the region and wanted to schedule a site visit early the following week. Would that be possible?

"Of course," Ben replied, thinking that she at least seemed friendly, not officious.

"Then how about Monday morning?"

"That would be fine," he heard himself saying, "see you then."

Ben set the phone down, crossed his arms, and looked from his aunt to his father, who had just joined them on the porch.

"Well, this will be interesting," was all he could muster.

"Don't be so down, son. We've always been fine," Grant, his father, said. "We'll get through it."

"No, we won't," Ben countered. "We barely did the last time, and we didn't make any of their recommendations, remember? They wanted the lobby carpeting replaced, the parking lot paved. . . . "

"As long as our satisfaction scores are in the ballpark, we'll be OK," Shirley said. "We've always had a loyal clientele. The new hotels around here can't say that; they don't have our history."

"History just means old," was Ben's reply.

The Company

Known for its well-kept, older properties for family and leisure travelers, Rest Easy Hotels is a popular, well-regarded regional franchise of the Amity Group. When the Amity Group was founded in 1950, it began with its own flagship chain of Amity Hotels. However, over the years it broadened its focus to include franchising and acquiring hotel brands if the price was right and renovation reasonable. Amity Group acquired the Rest Easy Hotel franchise in 1985.

The Amity Group actively partners with franchisees in the presentation and marketing of its brands. The group employs some 800 staff at its corporate headquarters, which relocated to the south a decade ago, and 2,000 hotel properties among seven brands. It has an annual revenue of more than $750 million.

"Is building loyalty building a business?"

Ben is a third-generation manager of his family's hotel. His grand-mother, to support her young family, bought the hotel, one of the franchise, in the 1960s with insurance money after her husband's death. And it has been a successful family enterprise. Ben's father and aunt studied hotel management at the state university and took over in the 1980s. They both raised families on the hotel property and continued to live there while working part time to support the business. Ben took over the hotel 10 years ago. Although his college degree is in English, he grew up in the hotel business, and everyone in the area knows him. He's a familiar fixture at the hotel, always with a book in hand and an easy manner.

When Ben's grandmother ran the hotel, she counted on developing personal relationships to grow her business, supported by returning business travelers, vacationers, and a variety of other visitors, such as parents and students visiting the area's many colleges. Hers was a quaint offering, the first hotel in the town itself, with other small hotels and bed-and-breakfasts scattered amid the surrounding mountain ranges and resorts.

By the time Grant and Shirley took over in the eighties, a renovation in the town center had led to an influx of hotels, offering travelers more choices. Business began to level off. Although the hotel could still support them, the family realized that passively waiting for business to come their way was a thing of the past. About this time, the Amity Group purchased the Rest Easy franchise, and Ben's father and aunt began professionalizing and modernizing the hotel. They also made an effort to broaden the range of amenities to compete with other hotels' offerings.

But the hotel had slipped during Ben's management. And, after some unenthusiastic online customer reviews during the past year, the corporate office discussed lowering the hotel's guest satisfaction score.

Ben often considered whether the hotel would benefit from more and better on-property management. In management parlance, their small, family-run business required a larger skill set than the family possessed. His father and aunt were now in their 60s, and while they were in good health, Ben would be the first to admit that the hotel had become very casual about customer service. Guests often reported waiting at length at the empty reception desk, and Ben couldn't be everywhere at once.

This attitude, Ben knew, stemmed in part to their beginnings as a family-friendly, casual stop—"where friends sent friends," which had become their motto. And over the years, guests did become family friends; some had even helped out with hotel renovations. But had loyalty made the family resistant to change? Loyalty to friends could have two sides. It was no longer unusual for a summer regular with a longstanding reservation to cancel with little or no notice, and Ben, who might have just turned away a prospective guest, would be left frustrated and with rooms to fill.

The family was also on the fence about his desire to make changes.

"I don't know about this step, honey," Shirley had said when he'd floated an idea about changing their reservation policy. "It seems like we're turning our backs on the people who've helped us the most over the years."

"You mean the horse show folks who sneak extras into their rooms without paying and leave mud all over the place?" Ben asked.

"Well, that's a tough one," she said. "We probably don't have the staff to keep after guests who are such a . . . challenge."

"We clearly can't count on building loyalty anymore; we've got to think about building a business," Ben muttered to no one in particular.

*　*　*

So Ben finally ended the hotel policy of holding groups of rooms for the summer regulars, the horse show people, the wedding planners, and all the rest. It would be first come, first served. But fewer and fewer came.

And now there was talk of an upscale hotel chain moving in across the street, the first one to come to town in more than a decade. Ben knew the prospective owners—they were the family of a close college friend, and had been waiting for such an opportunity for years. Ben wanted to be happy for his friend's family, but he was conflicted.

When Amity Group suggested the performance consultant visit to make some suggestions about staff and training, he balked, unsure whether such solutions could solve the hotel's growing problems. They'd long ago lost the only staff they had to retirement and were struggling to replace them—the local applicant pool of earlier years was simply gone. Ben and his family were both hotel owners and staff. These days they both ran the front desk and cleaned toilets.

It frustrated Ben when corporate headquarters further suggested that if he could elevate his customer satisfaction score by 15 percent, it would net about $50,000 additional income, allowing him to make some of the requested infrastructure repairs. It seemed so easy, in their view. But the fact was, the score was closer to slipping by 2 percent, which could invite remedial training or even the eventual loss of control of the property.

"We've always been fine."

Jamie, the performance consultant, was punctual, cordial, and helpful, although direct. How could she avoid asking about the shabby lobby carpeting or the ruts in the parking lot—the things he hadn't done—which had only gotten worse? But she also surprised him.

"I've seen great service with a poor product, and poor service with a great one," she said. "Our studies bear it out, too. The general manager sets the tone."

"Look, we've always been fine," Ben said. "Now you're saying it's all on me."

"Of course," she said, smiling. "But that's good, right? That means it's under your control."

"But I have a friend who wants to develop right across the street," Ben gestured with exasperation. "That's out of my control."

"I've heard about them. They'll quickly price themselves out of this market. That's not your competition. Besides, if I were them, I'd think about buying your place. You've created a renovator's dream. Is that what you want?"

Sell the hotel? His family would never sell. But would he?

For as long as he could remember, Ben's entire family was within earshot for dinner, every night. Now that could change.

TAKE 1

Commentary by Alan De Back

Alan De Back is a career counselor and learning consultant with more than 20 years of experience. He has served as director of global learning for an Internet consulting firm and manager of leadership development for a major aerospace corporation.

Traditional, family-run organizations often run into issues around being too casual in their management and not adapting to a changing marketplace. Ben's challenges reflect what so often happens in these types of organizations.

The major problems in this scenario are very much related to resistance to change and change management.

Ben is struggling with the values and culture of a long family history in managing the business. With little competition in the hotel's earlier years, the family had the luxury of a very casual management style with limited structure. In addition, his father and aunt still have a major influence on the business, and although they mean well, they are resistant to making changes to the hotel's roots. Ben seems to see some need for change, but is somewhat handcuffed by the other family members in the business.

Because the hotel has traditionally been a family-run business, another major issue is the family trying to do everything themselves. Although the case study mentions that there's no local applicant pool to hire staff members, there is little evidence that the family has really tried to find the staff they need. Customer service is definitely suffering as the family tries to fill all the roles themselves.

The hotel would benefit from some new and different approaches to running the business. First and foremost, communication needs to improve between Ben, his father, and his aunt. Although they seem to have a good personal relationship, communication seems limited when it comes to discussing the operation of the business. Grant and Shirley seem reluctant to make any changes, either major or minor, and Ben appears to be acquiescing to their wishes. He does seem to understand the need for change, but is either unwilling or unable to challenge his family.

Ben should view the performance consultant as an ally rather than an adversary. Jamie clearly understands the business and the challenges that exist. If Ben were less resistant, she could be valuable in helping him to turn the business around.

I would recommend that Ben have an open and honest conversation with his family members about the issues they are facing and what their course of action needs to be. He should carefully prepare for this conversation, and a book like *Crucial Conversations* (Patterson et al. 2012) would probably be helpful. Involving the performance consultant in the conversation might have some merit, but he should carefully prepare for a conversation with her as well.

After the conversation, Ben and his family must adopt a more businesslike approach to running the hotel. Although they have historically viewed their guests as "family," that approach no longer works in the 21st century. They can still strive to provide exceptional customer service, but they must realize that their guests are business clients.

Ben is struggling with the values and culture of a long family history in managing the business.

There is no evidence that Ben has any kind of business plan or vision for the hotel, and the operation seems to just be running on a day-to-day basis. Developing a business plan with a vision and goals is an important part of this more businesslike approach.

Related to all of this, customer service must become a priority. The hotel's customer service ratings have slipped because of issues such as no one working the front desk. Ben needs to hire staff members immediately to take over some of these responsibilities. Working with a recruiting agency might be worth the cost. If the labor pool is indeed very tight, an alternative might be to at least partially staff with interns or co-op students from a university that has a hospitality program.

Finally, it's not clear what kind of advertising the family has been using to promote the hotel. In the past, they apparently relied on returning guests to fill their rooms. With added competition, however, Ben needs to develop a publicity strategy. For example, an ad campaign can still relate to the family warmth that was the franchise's trademark in the past, but with a modern approach to running the business.

As for recommended resources, the performance consultant is one resource that Ben should take advantage of. She clearly understands the hospitality business and could be a great help. Rather than avoiding her and dreading her visits, I would suggest that Ben regularly reach out to her. If there is a nearby university, there could be opportunities for a group of students to come in, particularly at the graduate level, to do an analysis and make recommendations. Because the students would provide a fresh perspective not clouded by history, their recommendations could be very creative and useful as Ben develops his business plan.

TAKE 2

Commentary by Rick Rittmaster

Rick Rittmaster is the manager of learning and development at MTS, a global supplier of high-performance test systems and sensors.

This case study presents a handful of competing issues: The business lacks direction to operate effectively, there is a lack of clear roles and responsibilities, and resources are constrained. Progress on any one of these issues would probably translate to progress on other issues as well. However, I think that the main problem, and where to start, is that of Ben and his (in)ability to lead the Rest Easy Hotel. He has two primary challenges: leadership capability and his internal motivations toward his role at his family hotel.

Of the two, I believe Ben's internal motivation is the more pressing topic. At the beginning of the case, Ben is literally avoiding a hard truth, and it seems as though the full extent of that "hard truth" extends far beyond a nervous outlook on the future of the business. His avoidance indicates other, deeper reservations about his engagement with the hotel. Some data points to consider: He studied English and not hotel management, his family has been a constant presence and influence in his life, and the hotel has been slipping under his management.

Less than a third of family businesses survive the transition from first- to second-generation ownership, and another 50 percent don't survive the transition from second to third generation (Aileron 2013). Ben would likely still have some significant challenges, even if he was fully engaged in his role.

Ben can probably be developed into a competent leader; his current capabilities are a liability, but he can still see problems and formulate some minor plans. His most significant issue, and the biggest thing holding the hotel back, is a lack of motivation around leading the organization forward. To be blunt, he has to "want it," and it isn't clear if he really does. I would encourage him to get curious about other

Less than a third of family businesses survive the transition from first- to second-generation ownership.

options to help the hotel move forward. For example:

- What does the performance consultant think are other possible solutions?
- What immediate options does Ben have to improve the customer service?
- What have other hotels in a similar situation done (benchmarking)?
- Should the family consider outright selling?

Additionally, for the performance consultant, is there any information that would address some of the previously raised questions about Ben's motivation? To expand on this topic, it would also be helpful to understand the family's willingness and commitment to adjust and adapt to turn the business around.

I think Ben would need some type of coaching to determine what his role would be for the hotel, and whether he is interested in leading it through these changes. Ben seems to be his own worst enemy; it is critical that he be aware of what he does and doesn't want from the hotel before he tries to lead the organization forward.

Ben's path forward most likely won't be easy, but at least there are many paths to choose from. My recommendation is simple: Figure out if you want to lead. I'm critical of leaders who aren't willing to equally embrace the opportunity and the challenges of leadership. It is true that leadership is anything but easy. It is also true that leadership is even more difficult within a family business. However, Ben's inaction is dangerous.

Assuming that Ben remains in place for the foreseeable future, and assuming that the family decides to maintain the management of the hotel, I would encourage action around some type of "quick win" solution. Whether it is replacing the carpeting in the lobby, improving the service at the front desk, or even another option (free Wi-Fi, for example), the hotel needs some success that can act as a momentum-builder. This case conveys a general sense of heaviness, a lack of motivation to make any progress. With one victory comes the potential for more victories, which is why I think a quick win could be important.

Next, it would be helpful to engage in some dialogue with Ben, his father, and his aunt. It would be helpful to get clarity in terms of the organization's purpose and critical issues. The intent would be to get the three on the same page on why the hotel exists, and the main challenges that limit the current success. I would start by interviewing Ben, Grant, and Shirley independently, and then use that content to compile a short overview of the current situation to guide a group discussion and get alignment around these topics.

It would also be helpful to gain clarity regarding Grant and Shirley's long-term relationship with the hotel, and what they see as a successful outcome. My strongest recommendation would be to determine the overall appetite for change, and clarify how they can meaningfully support the changes. I'd bias solutions to support change around helping Ben more successfully lead the organization, as that is the more sustainable path forward for the hotel.

To be certain, there are resources and tools that can help the Rest Easy Hotel. The nuance is that this is a family business, and family businesses often have "quirks" that necessitate a different approach to traditional resources and tools. Often, it is easy for solutions to come across as too formal or heavy-handed. The performance consultant is a prime example of what I would call a typical reaction to what in other situations is a normal solution.

Assuming that the family is interested in genuinely discussing a strategy to move forward, I would consider using some type of small business effectiveness audit. These usually look at a variety of topics and allow for scoring to determine the current effectiveness and level of impact. The specific audit isn't important, but I would recommend one focusing on internal processes, people and talent capabilities, leadership capabilities, and the ability to meet customer needs.

I've found success in similar situations by subtly weaving in aspects of different solutions. For example, I might ask a subset of audit questions without prompting the leader, then let the conversation open up into a broader discussion that is more aligned with a formal audit. But in the case of this hotel, it is more a function of how the resources or tools are introduced and applied, rather than what specifically that tool or resource can do.

I have had the opportunity to both work for a family business and provide some coaching and consulting for family businesses, and in almost all instances the issue of family ties was a significant factor. So, unfortunately, I believe this is a common scenario. To avoid this problem, the Rest Easy Hotel must be crystal clear in its purpose: What is the value it provides? Who are the main customers? Why should the organization continue to exist? Answering these questions would be a significant step toward determining solutions and a path forward.

In addition, organizations can benefit tremendously from setting clear roles and responsibilities. Often this can feel bureaucratic in a small organization. However, the absence of roles and responsibilities, especially in a family-owned business, leads to confusion, misaligned expectations, and poor performance. Small organizations and family businesses often expect employees to wear many hats. To continue to support this culture, roles and responsibilities can outline primary and backup responsibilities. For this family-run hotel, I imagine it would be important to balance a general sense of helping when and where help is needed, and creating clearer expectations with better defined responsibilities.

Overall, the strongest recommendation I have for Ben and his family is to simply listen to those around them and take advantage of the help being offered. If you're struggling to stay afloat, don't be too choosy about which life preserver you grab.

9

NEW COLLEGE DIRECTOR SEES ONLY FACULTY MYOPIA

Cast of Characters at Westdale College

Andrew Miller—New Director of the Executive Leadership Program
Tom Ryan, PhD—Faculty Adviser
Sarah Mack—HR Director

"Stop by My Office"

From a distance, the ivy-covered, elevated red-brick walkway connecting the two classic campus administration buildings created harmony, serenity, and balance. In the afternoon, sunlight filtered through as students and faculty walked under the leafy canopy. It was 500 feet, 125 paces. Andrew Miller knew this because he walked it several times a week, sometimes twice a day. That was because his office was in one building, and Tom Ryan's office was in the other. As the new director of the college's Executive Leadership Program, Andrew often found himself needing to talk to Dr. Ryan, the program's faculty adviser. Unfortunately, he rarely answered his office phone or email, and didn't have a cell. He did have an assistant, but she didn't know his daily schedule other than what he posted on the office door at the beginning of each quarter.

Dr. Ryan often told Andrew to stop by his office. Whenever they ran into each other on the small campus and Andrew would try to talk about some aspect of the program, Dr. Ryan would interrupt him to say earnestly, "Stop by my office this afternoon. We'll set something up. I look forward to it."

So far, Andrew had found him in his office exactly twice—both times with a half-dozen students waiting to talk to him. He had yet to get an appointment.

Executive Leadership Program

The Executive Leadership Program at Westdale College was established 30 years ago in partnership with regional business and industry leaders seeking to develop executive leadership within their predominantly manufacturing community. The certification program, which was created and taught by cross-disciplinary scholars and business faculty, included topical themes explored in small-class seminars. A five-member faculty board, drawn primarily from the business school, supported and advised the dean of business programs and extracurricular studies, who had direct oversight of the ELP.

Originally, the program's students were employees of the region's businesses, and for years there was a steady flow of professional students, primarily managers and executives. But over the last two decades, outsourcing and recession had decimated the local manufacturing businesses and, consequently, the ELP. When they left town, two major industries withdrew from the program, and now the latest student numbers were half of what they used to be.

In its current state, the program needed both an infusion of funding and students from new business partners; the faculty board was also reconsidering its mission to reach out to both international and regional partners from nonprofits, healthcare, education, and government.

"I Have No Boss"

Andrew had been hired at the end of the last school year. At 35, he was younger and less experienced than many directors of such programs nationwide, but he had come highly recommended by the last program director and dean, who had met him at a winter weekend leadership conference. Andrew had attended as the representative of the Business Leaders Seminars Program at his university, where he was the assistant director. It was a larger program than Westdale's and had wide-ranging business support; it had also recently received a significant alumni endowment.

Andrew had not been looking for a new position, but he was flattered to think others thought he could lead their program, so he agreed to tour Westdale. When he visited the campus the following spring, he met the five faculty board members, all long-tenured in the business school, who advised and supported the Executive Leadership Program. Each interviewed Andrew at length, and then hosted him at a friendly lunch at the faculty dining hall. Andrew felt that he'd been well prepared for the interview, and had come with many questions about the program, especially concerning its viability. He found the faculty congenial and forthcoming, open and inquisitive about his suggestions. All his questions had been answered to his satisfaction. In his view, the faculty board seemed open to change and new perspectives. Excited about the position, he took the job.

But things quickly changed that fall. Within six weeks of his arrival, Andrew was ready to quit out of sheer frustration. In his opinion, little of what the faculty board members had said during his interview turned out to be true.

This was complicated by the fact that the dean he was supposed to report to was on leave, and it was unclear if or when she would return.

She had sent Andrew an email a few weeks before the semester started, mentioning medical tests that would keep her off campus when he first arrived, but now, according to the business school's dean, she might be gone the entire semester. The dean had also mentioned that they'd asked Dr. Ryan to act in her place, but from what Andrew could tell, he wasn't. Andrew was feeling the burden of no reporting structure.

One of Andrew's earliest business lessons was from his father, with whom he talked often, about his first job after business school. "I was a young assistant product manager with a top national household products manufacturer," his father recalled. "I had no boss, no one to report to. The entire time I was there, I never got a boss. People moved around a lot, some just left, so it seemed possible they could have just lost track of me."

"Maybe they thought you were so smart you didn't need a boss?"

"Well, one day, one of the more senior people took me aside and basically said just that—and then he was gone. His way of saying goodbye."

"What's the moral of that story?"

"Sometimes, being smart isn't enough," his father said. "There's more that goes into having the tools to do the job."

"The Party of No"

Andrew stopped in to see the college's HR director, Sarah Mack, who confirmed what he suspected—that the dean hadn't been well and was taking some needed time-off for prospective surgery and recuperation. A new dean would be appointed soon, but perhaps not until the second semester.

"I'm sorry if it appears we're not prepared for you," Sarah said. "Obviously, the Excellence in Leadership Program needs your direction, so please understand that we really are glad you're here."

Andrew, grateful for Sarah's words, pressed on. He was elated when the faculty board agreed to his proposal to expand the number of international applicants, but frustrated when they cut his funding for recruitment. The Mexican partnership model he'd described in his interview, which they'd responded to positively, they now said was unfeasible. He got the same response about a Canadian university group he'd eyed for a prospective partnership.

When Andrew proposed restructuring student-faculty meeting days to include Saturdays, half the faculty objected, saying it would interfere with their regular tennis league. At first Andrew thought they must be joking—refusing to consider a program improvement because of a tennis conflict—but he was astonished to learn that it was no joke. Frustrated, he knew that just outside campus were the program's severely contracted former business partners, all of whom could no longer support them. The business school needed to find a way to engage the next generation of students with both real-time and virtual learning. The problem as Andrew saw it was that the faculty taught all the best management practices but didn't follow them. Was there a disconnect between the business school, its comfortable leafy campus enclave, and the shuttered factories on the other side of town?

"I've begun calling them the party of no," Andrew told his father.

"People don't start out that way," his father replied. "But over time, surrounded by like-minded others, they could appear to run their program successfully without oversight or scrutiny. The question for you is, what do you do now?"

At this point, Andrew had no authority to make changes in the program he directed, and no influence over those who did. He felt rudderless.

Good News?

Sarah delivered the news in a folded message tacked to his door—an interim dean had been appointed and would be on campus before the end of the semester. "Good news, right?" she'd scrawled in apparent haste across the bottom.

But Andrew had just received a group email message from the interim dean: "Looking forward to being back on campus with my old ELP friends. Is tennis league still on Saturdays?"

TAKE 1

Commentary by Christopher D. Adams

Christopher D. Adams is a performance consultant and instructional designer with more than 20 years' experience helping clients engage people, apply processes, and implement technology to improve human and organizational performance.

The main issue in this case is likely the one Andrew feels most strongly: He has the responsibility for building and maintaining a program, but no authority to take the actions needed to ensure success. To be effective, he will need the support and cooperation of a client team—the board and sponsoring dean (when that dean is back in place). But in his short time on the job, he does not seem to have taken effective actions to develop that client-team relationship. Here is an approach that I believe could help Andrew moving forward.

First, Andrew needs to stop focusing on the means, or solutions, and start focusing on the desired ends. It is certainly understandable that Andrew feels left to his own devices. The semester is already under way, so faculty time is scarce; the sponsoring dean is absent due to health concerns; and there are negative trends that make the future of the Executive Leadership Program uncertain. Andrew clearly wants to be proactive in taking quick action to immediately improve the program. Unfortunately, this leads him to an early focus on the means before the ends, and the various factors that affect them, are fully established.

One detail from the case indicating that Andrew lacks a full understanding of how needs around the program align is his proposal to restructure student-faculty meeting days to include Saturdays. While this suggests a strong student focus, it meets with resistance from the board because it's a solution that doesn't consider the needs of the faculty.

Conducting a needs assessment would help Andrew begin with ends rather than means. In such an assessment, he could gather data from representatives of stakeholder groups at a number of levels. Students, certainly, but also ELP faculty and staff members, board members, alumni, and program applicants. Sponsoring business leaders could even provide insight as to the needs of the larger community the college serves. This effort need not take excessive amounts of time—just a matter of a few weeks—and then Andrew could present this data to the board.

Second, Andrew needs to lead any proposals with data. At one point in the case, he becomes frustrated because the Mexican partnership model he first suggested during his interview process was deemed unfeasible. This was apparently a solution that worked well at the larger university where he worked previously. But, though the idea of this partnership model was well received during his interview—likely because it was an indicator of his knowledge and related experience—the actual solution was not seen as a fit for Westdale by the board.

Instead of presenting a raft of solutions to the board—simply hoping they'd be well received—Andrew may have fared better if he first presented data from a needs assessment. This would have built agreement and a shared understanding of the goals for the ELP based on stakeholder needs and the barriers to achieving those goals. Once he established this agreement, Andrew would have increased his credibility with the board and better informed his own ideas about what solutions were appropriate.

Although it seems from the case that Andrew put means before ends in his interactions with the board thus far, it is not too late for him to begin leading with data. He can use the feedback from the board as the first data points in his assessment of needs related to the ELP.

Once he has given the board some data, Andrew should engage the board in the process of selecting appropriate solutions, rather than immediately advocating for his own. Consultants influence far more by what they ask than what they tell. This could certainly be true for Andrew. By asking how each barrier to the agreed-upon goals might be addressed, he can surface any remaining concerns and generate additional ideas for solutions that the board is willing to support. In doing so, he's making the board his client team.

Of course, Andrew should have his own suggestions for appropriate solutions aligned with each barrier and goal. But offering them in the context of this conversation improves the likelihood he can influence the board to take action. For example, there is faculty resistance to Saturday meetings with students, but perhaps the board would be willing to add an adjunct position to allow for more flexibility. Or, the faculty members who don't play tennis might be willing to cover student meetings on Saturdays in exchange for some other consideration during weekday hours. These are solutions that would be difficult for Andrew to plan and propose on his own, but which are easily implemented in partnership with a client team.

If Andrew can successfully focus on ends before means, lead with data, and influence by asking, he should be in a position to begin implementing a set of appropriate solutions, backed by the support of his dean and the board. At that point, he could also begin working to better align the authority he has to take action with the responsibility he's been given. After all, based on the data he gathered, he and the board have agreed to goals that must be met and the board has provided input on actions to be taken. Moving forward, Andrew might reasonably ask that, within an established budget and timeline, he be given authority to execute the agreed-upon actions without needing board approval for each action in

Consultants influence far more by what they ask than what they tell.

detail. Andrew will be responsible for evaluating the effectiveness of the agreed-upon solutions and updating the board periodically—but won't be required to overcome a chorus of nos at every step.

TAKE 2

Commentary by Sharlyn Lauby

Sharlyn Lauby is the president of ITM Group and author of the blog HR Bartender.

In my experience, the culture of higher education is unique. So, there could be organizational structures and traditions in play that don't relate to other industries. That being said, there are a couple of aspects to this scenario that many industries will find relevant.

In this case study, Andrew has the title, office, and the responsibility. The question is, does he have the authority? A person who has responsibility without authority is destined to fail.

I'm curious to know what conversations took place between Andrew and the dean during the recruiting process. I'm a big fan of collaborative hiring, because having multiple people involved in the recruiting process gives new hires several people they can turn to when they have questions (and don't necessarily want to go to their boss or HR for answers).

Was the dean aware of what was taking place within the ELP's faculty board (that is, the tennis league environment)? If so, was that communicated to Andrew? I don't get the impression that Andrew picked up on the faculty board dynamic during his interviews and lunch with them, but did the dean offer any hints? Is the faculty board camaraderie a well-kept secret?

There are two approaches I would initially consider—one for Andrew and the other for the college.

First, if I were Andrew, I would step back and take a very objective approach to this situation. I would think about what took place during the interview process. Were there signs I should have noticed? Questions I could have asked but didn't? I would also ask myself if this is a problem I'm prepared to deal with. It's not clear how much (or little) Andrew likes this job or the college. Those responses could answer a lot of questions.

At some point, Andrew will need to confront his lack of authority. He took the job based on a set of assumptions and, according to his account, it sounds like he was bamboozled. If he doesn't get the authority to do his job, he will continue to be frustrated, which could lead him to the point of leaving. Moreover, it could prevent him from accomplishing his goals of turning the program around (which would lead to his eventual dismissal).

Second, I'd like to think that human resources will reach out to Andrew for his feedback. He's a new employee with a fresh set of eyes, which gives him a valuable perspective to share. In addition, HR should also ask the faculty board for their feedback. They were part of the hiring process. We're assuming based on the case study that Andrew bears no responsibility in this situation. However, it would be interesting to know the faculty's perceptions, especially to Andrew's proposed changes.

Ultimately, the organization—that is, the dean and HR—need to make sure he is set up for success. He is a new employee and deserves a proper onboarding. The onboarding process also involves more than the dean, so others in the college—including the faculty board, which supposedly bought into Andrew being hired—should be making sure that Andrew is welcome and equipped for success. I would hope that the organization isn't too late, and Andrew hasn't already decided to start looking for a new opportunity.

The new interim dean, introduced at the end of the case study, will have to walk the tightrope of being friendly without being seen as a friend. If that line is crossed, it could be perceived as favoritism, which would hurt the interim dean's credibility and the college work environment overall. At this point, the interim dean's group email note might be harmless. It wouldn't be fair to judge. But it has the potential to be damaging.

In addition to new hire orientation and onboarding, the college should develop an onboarding program specifically for new managers. Managers are responsible for a lot and their success or failure can trickle down the organization. They should also conduct new hire feedback sessions and pulse surveys to make sure that new hires are getting the information and training they need to be successful. Short electronic surveys or one-on-one meetings can let the organization know when to adjust before employees get frustrated.

Unfortunately, organizations do sometimes leave out team and culture dynamics during the recruiting process. This isn't an issue exclusive to higher education. And it's not intentional. Companies want their workplace to come across as utopia so candidates will want to work there. Every organization has its challenges.

Organizations may leave out team dynamics when recruiting so they come across as utopia.

It's also unfortunate that organizations often do not give new employees a proper welcome. They assume that because the new employee is smart and competent they don't need any guidance. That's simply not true. This is exactly the reason onboarding programs are so important—even for senior-level positions. Organizations have unwritten rules. Giving new employees a buddy or a mentor can help share them.

10

MANEUVERING THE NEW HEALTHCARE

Cast of Characters at Eastlake General Hospital

Emily Fisher—Patient Care Representative

Tony Worley—Charge Nurse

Dr. Hans Jonas—Head of Wellness Institute

The Tower

Now that the Tower was finally complete, people were proud of the gleaming new 10-story addition to Eastlake General Hospital. It stood out like a beacon on the horizon, welcoming everyone who approached the hospital campus. It also doubled the hospital's square footage, adding desperately needed hospital beds. So it seemed almost counter-intuitive to Emily Fisher that now that the building was complete—and they no longer had to deal with the daily dust, rumble, vibration, or general disruption of a construction zone—she had begun hearing complaints from colleagues.

"Well, now that it's finished, we have patients in the Tower and have to go up there several times a day," Tony Worley, one of the charge nurses, told her. "It's not that we didn't know this would happen, but reality is a . . ."

"Don't say it," laughed Emily. "It's too early."

*　*　*

Emily was a patient care representative in the hospital's Wellness Institute, which had been her dream job when she started more than five years ago. With an advanced degree in public health, she wasn't a nurse like many of her hospital colleagues, but she believed she understood both their point of view and their pain. Tony wasn't the first nurse to point out that the Tower had added five miles and an extra hour to his daily rounds.

"I like the exercise," he would say, "and I don't have family waiting at home. But, what about the others?"

Emily knew whom he meant—the floor nurses who'd earlier taken in stride the move from eight- to 12-hour shifts, which were now stretching easily to 13 hours or longer. Some of those nurses were among the hospital's most experienced staff, and had planned to retire years ago before the recession changed their plans.

Eastlake General Hospital

Eastlake General Hospital, founded in the 1890s, was the city of Eastlake's first hospital. Its radiology department was one of the first such accredited departments in the country, and it has become known for advancements in geriatric medicine, hospice and palliative care, women's health, orthopedics, and cardiology. The 400-bed hospital remains top ranked in its region, a provider of compassionate healthcare from its original downtown location. At a cost of $300 million, the recently completed 10-story tower had added 70 private beds and five surgery theaters.

"Where's everybody going?"

On the other side of town, the new University Family Health Center (UFHC) opened on the old City Hospital grounds. It wasn't uncommon to hear of another nurse who'd left Eastlake to work there. Emily drove past it daily, watching as it grew from green space after the hospital was bulldozed to a brand-new facility. UFHC was part of the ambitious University Health Clinic, which had expanded its reach over the last decade adding locations throughout the region and boasting a renewed mission of patient care. It was also one of the first hospitals to create a new office of patient experience, which was tasked with actively using patient satisfaction surveys and technology.

The Wellness Institute, despite its name, wasn't on the same level. Dr. Hans Jonas, the institute's director and Emily's boss, meant well; he was an earnest practitioner, but not dynamic. He was older, but the problem wasn't his age, it was his personality. To put it bluntly, she wondered whether his temperament was suited for healthcare at all. He'd been reprimanded for his dealings with nurses and was often sharp with any staff on the hospital floor. He had been associated with the hospital his entire career, and when the administration transitioned from medical specialties to institutes and departments, Dr. Jonas was made director of the Wellness Institute. However, as the last one created, it almost seemed like an afterthought—and many wondered if it was a means to sideline Dr. Jonas or force him out.

The Institute was one of the hospital's smaller departments in terms of staff and budget, but Emily thought it had great potential for a wider reach in preventive care. Its full-time staff consisted of Dr. Jonas, a physiotherapist, a physician's assistant, a nurse practitioner, and Emily; it also contracted with private practitioners throughout the city who led a variety of classes and courses across the wellness spectrum. But Emily thought that not focusing its presence among patients during their hospital stay and after was a missed opportunity. She believed the Institute could have greater impact than it had among people at a critical healing time of their lives. She and Dr. Jonas had long had discussions about this, but they'd led nowhere, as far as she was concerned. Emily ultimately decided that as long as Dr. Jonas directed the Wellness Institute, its mission wouldn't change.

* * *

"Where's everybody going?" Dr. Jonas asked suddenly. It was the end of the work week, the offices were empty, and Tony had swung by at the end of his floor shift.

"Out for a drink. Wanna come?" Tony ventured. Emily glared at him.

Dr. Jonas looked at him, confused. "No, I mean . . . not that. Where's everybody on your floor going? It looks like you've lost nurses."

"Well, that's true," replied Tony. "Two have gone to that new family health center."

"How about you?"

"I don't mind my shifts, so I don't know. . . . But it's stressful losing people, for sure."

"So that's why people leave, because of their shifts?" Dr. Jonas asked.

"There's other reasons, too, but there's always a shiny new car."

Dr. Jonas looked at Tony blankly, and glanced at Emily, who stood in the doorway with her coat on, ready to go.

"The new place is pretty appealing," she said by way of explanation. "They're getting the hours they want, better pay, and it's very patient driven."

"Hmm, sounds like you've given that some thought," said Dr. Jonas.

"Disruption is good?"

When Emily was offered the new position of assistant director for patient care at UFHC, she waited a week before telling anyone at the hospital.

"Maybe you don't want it," Tony said matter of factly. "Maybe you're not ready to make that kind of move."

"No, I think I'm ready," she said. "This is the kind of position I was hoping we'd have here at the hospital by now. It just hasn't turned out that way."

So Emily was surprised when Dr. Jonas made her a counteroffer, asking her to create the kind of team that she thought the Wellness Institute needed.

"That would take money," she said.

"Which you wouldn't have, you know that," he said. "Budgets are tight, but you'd have my full support, which if you think about it, is still worth something."

"Look," Emily said, facing her boss, "Everything I read says disruption is coming to us here at the hospital, to healthcare, and that it's a good thing. And I say, really? Change is difficult. I think that I can have more impact in primary care because that's where the people are."

"Aren't people everywhere?" Dr. Jonas asked. "Try and figure out those things you've told me about. Why do people miss appointments? What about offering same-day appointments? Can you figure out a way to develop some teams across disciplines and get some answers? It would all be voluntary, of course, but I'll be behind you if you get results. What if it had effects in the hospital as well as beyond, wouldn't that be something?"

Emily had to admit that Dr. Jonas had given her something to think about. Should she accept his challenge, or leave for UFHC and a promotion?

TAKE 1

Commentary by Ben Locwin

Ben Locwin is CEO of a healthcare consulting organization. He has held executive roles for top pharmaceutical companies and developed human performance models for a variety of organizations.

Dr. Jonas seems to be the personification of "the old guard," where cemented mindsets don't allow innovation to match what the external environment is looking for—that is, a more personalized patient experience. I have had to field so many questions and conversations, and teach so many programs on patient-centricity over the past year, it almost seems like the patient was never even part of the primary care equation in the past. This is nonsense, of course, but with so many technological modalities pushing for personalization (such as choosing a show at the moment you want it with Netflix, or having meal boxes delivered to your door), the idea that as a patient, we can be put front and center in the process with personalized care has really taken off. It sounds great at face value; however, the issue is actually providing evidence-based care for patients in a way such that no one receives markedly better or worse care than anyone else. So the panacea of patient-centricity eventually meets up with the practical realities of healthcare systems serving millions of patients.

This case study begins by illustrating a focus more typical of business—creating an edifice (or edifices) designed to draw in new customers, yet with poor value propositions to keep the customers happy with the actual service. I've done work in hospitals where they tried to have better magazine subscriptions, HD TVs, faster Wi-Fi, better coffee machines, and so forth. But what the customers really want is better care and service, not better magazines. These efforts become wasted money.

Another case of dubious appropriation are the ubiquitous "patient surveys," referenced in this case as evidence of a "renewed mission of patient care." I have a colleague who had a fairly major surgery recently and, after being a patient for about five days, received a survey at home asking "how they did." His response was to throw it out, because "they simply did their job." With so much self-selection happening in the survey respondents (who will most likely return it only if they have strongly negative comments), the applicable usability of the surveys asymptomatically approaches zero.

Dr. Jonas doesn't have a clue how to manage the future of patient care in the Wellness Institute and is looking to have Emily be the point person for developing all new approaches, for which she'll receive almost none of the credit. It was a hollow offer from Dr. Jonas, most likely motivated by his fear of losing her. This isn't uncommon—in fact, every counteroffer ever proposed in business has been due to fear of losing good talent.

The Wellness Institute is already outsourcing to private practitioners, a management choice that makes it very difficult to rein in the variation in performance and practice within healthcare facilities. It's like running an operations center stocked with temps—they don't approach their work the same way; they don't feel the same social identity with the building, grounds, and staff; and they don't believe they need to adhere to "house rules."

Emily will have much more ability to grow and flourish in the new division of UFHC than she will sticking with Dr. Jonas. In all likelihood, he won't last much longer anyway if the strategic plan really was to push him to

Every counteroffer in business is made from fear of losing good talent.

the periphery so that he leaves. In that case, Emily will have to face this same decision again—and she may not have an open opportunity waiting for her then.

Further, if Emily does stay, and budgets shrink and she feels resentment toward Dr. Jonas, she'll feel like she had wasted all the time following her decision to stay. Typically, what motivates people to stay in "known" situations is fear of the unknown. Our brains are hardwired to give us alert signals if we're doing something that's out of our comfort zone. The alternative is to move on and face the associated uncertainties. This will seem to be a much riskier venture, but in this case, nothing could be further from the truth! The UFHC's facility seems welcoming to her, it is practicing the type of contemporary medicine that she seems to resonate with, and her status quo is likely to change in the not-too-distant future. Emily won't grow if she doesn't brave new experiences.

TAKE 2

Commentary by Glen B. Earl

Glen B. Earl is the department chair of the Industrial/Organizational Psychology Program for The Chicago School of Professional Psychology, Dallas, Texas, campus.

There are several main problems in this case study. With the new addition of the Tower, executives and builders did not take into consideration the effect it would have on employees. It just takes more time and energy to move to and from the new building. This is using up employee time and energy, which was already in short supply.

Today, healthcare is quickly moving to value over volume, care, and costs. Keeping patients healthy versus sick is better for hospital revenue, community wellness, and societal well-being. But the Wellness Institute described here appears to be an afterthought when it ought to be a primary part of the hospital.

Wellness, as Emily postulated, is a two-pronged approach. One prong focuses on the community and keeping patients healthy and out of the hospital. The other prong is patient care in the hospital and immediately afterward. In healthcare, a 30-day-or-less readmission for the same condition is viewed as a direct result of poor patient care by the hospital. Readmissions mean less revenue and a less positive patient experience.

There is also a poor job–person fit between the Wellness Institute and Dr. Jonas as its director. Wellness is now a medical specialty, with a primary care focus and a holistic view of the patient. At its current organizational stage, the Wellness Institute needs a dynamic staff, visionaries, missionaries, and evangelists to win over a staid, entrenched industry culture and the community's resource allocations, not to mention influence societal norms that perpetuate poor health habits.

Eastlake General Hospital has an outdated organizational culture and structure. Its executive leadership has the hospital focused on the old model of care (volume) instead of the future (value). There also seems to be little or no focus on reducing the increasing employee turnover. At least, the organization certainly does not appear to have a grasp on why their employees are leaving.

To better understand the problems at Eastlake, I'd like to examine voluntary turnover data, employee engagement scores, and patient experience data, as well as best practice comparison data to benchmark against.

Also, I'd like to have more information about the hospital's organizational culture, physician engagement, and comparison costs between the old and the new hospitals. The hospital's organizational chart and its strategic plan would be helpful, too. Furthermore, I would like to see the hospital's career-pathing process, employee development programs, and community outreach efforts.

One area not directly addressed in this case study is employee engagement, although the amount of employee turnover alludes to it. A tool and resource they could use is the employee engagement survey. These really affect two major populations: Higher employee engagement scores point to better results for employees and patients.

Patient experience is fast becoming a major focal point of patient care. In today's environment, government monetary reimbursement is directly tied to how patients feel about their overall hospital experience. Research consistently links employee engagement and patient experience (Press Ganey 2017). Further, considering that many patient experiences have the potential to be negative by their very nature, hospitals are more and more aware of positively affecting patient visits in any way they can, including examining employee beliefs and mindsets (Hess 2017). Unhappy patients will share more than those who are satisfied (Baird 2014).

Saying that, my first recommendation to Emily is to stop listening to Dr. Jonas's offer, give her two-week notice, and leave. He is giving her weak promises, even conceding that there would be no more money and extra, voluntary work. And, he indicated that he would stand behind her only if she gets results; that's not much of a counteroffer.

As for Eastlake, I would recommend focusing on the employee experience and engagement, as well as the patient experience. Further, I would recommend that it focus on its future, what it will take to get there, and what type of organizational structure, culture, and employee type it will take to get it to its new state.

Regarding other staff, where are the senior and middle managers? These groups translate the vision into day-to-day operations, which is a critically important task. Middle management, when armed with courage, compassion,

Unhappy patients will share more than those who are satisfied.

and candor, can become a mighty force for positive organizational change. It is the fulcrum by which an organization is moved.

This is a very common scenario in healthcare. Healthcare systems are ever changing—consolidating here, expanding there. In particular, as older hospitals build new additions, the added square footage significantly affects a clinical employee's work life. The sheer increase in the amount of walking by bedside clinicians is legendary.

There is always increased turnover when hospitals go through renovations. Many staff decide to leave before the new hospital opens, especially employees who are near retirement. A big part of their rationale is not wanting to deal with all the new technology. Another wave of turnover occurs after the new building opens. Employees gain some experience and may decide, "This is not for me." When Dallas-based Parkland Hospital moved into its new building, it prepared for expected increased turnover before and after the move by delivering a change-management class to more than 5,000 clinical personnel.

A healthcare organization can avoid many if not all negative issues in this case study. One of the first changes is to move from a hierarchical organizational structure to a more flexible, decentralized one. This gives personnel and work units the freedom and flexibility to make real, just-in-time decisions that affect their local area or work process and product, which are not related to other parts of the organization.

Another action is to assess the organization's positive deviants. A positive deviant is a department or work unit that excels in the same environment where other personnel and work units do not. Eastlake General Hospital has several areas of excellence, including radiology, geriatric medicine, hospice and palliative care, women's health, orthopedics, and cardiology. A root cause analysis could help them assess why and how these areas excel, so they could try to replicate it throughout the rest of the hospital.

REFERENCES AND RESOURCES

Accenture. 2013. "U.S. Employees Eager to be Corporate Entrepreneurs but Lack Support and Rewards from Employers, Accenture Research Finds." News release. December 16. https://newsroom.accenture.com /news/us-employees-eager-to-be-corporate-entrepreneurs-but-lack -support-and-rewards-from-employers-accenture-research-finds.htm.

Aileron. 2013. "The Facts of Family Business." *Forbes,* July 31. www.forbes .com/sites/aileron/2013/07/31/the-facts-of-family-business/#5ea34f3a9884.

Allis, R. "How to Solve Big Problems." The Startup Guide. http://startup guide.com/entrepreneurship/find-a-big-problem.

American Society for Quality (ASQ). 2017. "Learn About Quality: Pareto Chart." http://asq.org/learn-about-quality/cause-analysis -tools/overview/pareto.html.

ATD (Association for Talent Development). 2017. "Training vs. Performance Consulting (Part 2): The Analysis (Speaker: Joe Willmore)." Human Capital Podcasts, December 7. https://videos.td.org/detail /videos/human-capital-podcasts/video/5363318840001/training-vs. -performance-consulting-part-2-:-the-analysis-focus?.

Atkinson, W. 2008. "Getting Lean and Going Green: Innovations in Warehouse Operations." *Inbound Logistics,* May 15. www.inbound logistics.com/cms/article/getting-lean-and-going-green-innovations -in-warehouse-operations.

Bagai, S. 2016. "Individualized Retention Efforts Work Best." *The Buzz,* July 28. Association for Talent Development. www.td.org/newsletters /the-buzz/individualized-retention-efforts-work-best.

Baird, K. 2014. "Engaged, Empowered and Enthused: The Link Between Employee Engagement and the Patient Experience." *Becker's Hospital Review,* January 9. www.beckershospitalreview.com/hospital-manage ment-administration/engaged-empowered-and-enthused-the-link -between-employee-engagement-and-the-patient-experience.html.

Blade, V.H. 2016. "Gaining Experience and Moving Up." Chapter 13 in *Find Your Fit: A Practical Guide to Landing a Job You'll Love,* edited by S. Kaiden. Alexandria, VA: ATD Press.

Bort, J. 2013. "The 15 Most Valuable Cloud Computing Companies in the World Are Worth Way More Than You'd Think." *Business Insider,* July 29. www.businessinsider.com/the-15-most-valuable-cloud -computing-companies-2013-7.

BPI (Business Performance Improvement). 2014. "Lean Manufacturing and Six Sigma Definitions: Glossary, Terms and Definitions for Lean and Six Sigma: 5S." BPI. http://leansixsigmadefinition.com/glossary/5s.

Bray, M.W. 2016. "How to Turn Your Average Warehouse into a Power-house." *Distribution Center Magazine,* June 27. www.distribution centermag.com/articles/85421-how-to-turn-your-average-warehouse -into-a-powerhouse.

Bruzzese, A. 2014. "On the Job: How to Encourage Innovation in Your Company." *USA Today,* January 5. www.usatoday.com/story/money /columnist/bruzzese/2014/01/05/on-the-job-encourage-innovation /4285947.

Bulygo, Z. 2013. "The 4 Elements That Make Great Company Culture." *Kissmetrics Blog,* January 25. https://blog.kissmetrics.com/great -company-culture.

Byrne, K., and J. Detert. 2005. *Business Cycles and Employment Practices in a Domestic Garment Company (A).* Business Roundtable Institute for Corporate Ethics. www.corporate-ethics.org/pdf/BRI -1002A.pdf.

Carnegie Mellon Tepper School of Business. 2015. *Arthur Andersen Case Studies in Business Ethics.* June 4. http://public.tepper.cmu.edu/ethics /AA/arthurandersen.htm.

Claman, P. 2014. "How to Get Out from Under Your Boss's Shadow." *Harvard Business Review,* December 2. https://hbr.org/2014/12 /how-to-get-out-from-under-your-bosss-shadow.

Cohn, A. 2016. "Developing Your Career Plan." Chapter 4 in *Find Your Fit: A Practical Guide to Landing a Job You'll Love,* edited by S. Kaiden. Alexandria, VA: ATD Press.

Coleman, M. 2011. "Safety and Warehouse Storage." *Occupational Health & Safety Online,* August 1. https://ohsonline.com/articles /2011/08/01/safety-and-warehouse-storage.aspx.

Collins, J. 2001. *Good to Great: Why Some Companies Make the Leap . . . and Others Don't.* New York: HarperCollins.

Curtis, B., B. Hefley, and S. Miller. 2009. *People Capability Maturity Model,* 2nd edition. Hanscom AFB, MA: Software Engineering Institute.

Dale Carnegie. "Engaged Employees Infographic." www.dalecarnegie.com /employee-engagement/engaged-employees-infographic.

Dannecker, J. 2015. "10 Ideas for More Efficient & Productive Warehouse Operations." *Cerasis,* March 5. http://cerasis.com/2015/03/05 /warehouse-operations.

Donovan, J., and C. Benko. 2016. "AT&T's Talent Overhaul." *Harvard Business Review,* October. https://hbr.org/2016/10/atts-talent-overhaul.

Douglas, M. 2015. "The Changing Face of the Warehouse Workforce." *Inbound Logistics,* May 20. www.inboundlogistics.com/cms/article /the-changing-face-of-the-warehouse-workforce.

Elbein, S. 2014. "When Employees Confess, Sometimes Falsely." *New York Times,* March 8. www.nytimes.com/2014/03/09/business /when-employees-confess-sometimes-falsely.html.

Ellet, W. 2007. *The Case Study Handbook: How to Read, Discuss, and Write Persuasively About Cases.* Boston: Harvard Business School Publishing.

Feldstein, M., and S. Kaiden. 2016. "Should I Stay or Should I Go? How Happy Are You at Work?" *ATD Insights,* September 8. www.td.org /insights/should-i-stay-or-should-i-go.

Major Gifts Officer. 2013. "First Person Nonprofit: A Day in the Life of a Major Gifts Officer." *Blue Avocado,* December 13. www.blueavocado .org/content/first-person-nonprofit-day-life-major-gifts-officer.

Gallup. n.d. "StrengthsFinder/CliftonStrengths." www.gallupstrengths center.com/home/en-US/Index.

Gartner. 2016. "Talent Assessment." July 17. www.cebglobal.com /talent-management/talent-assessment.html%20.html.

Gilbert, T. 2007. *Human Competence: Engineering Worthy Performance.* San Francisco: Pfeiffer.

Harter, J., and B. Rigoni. 2015. *The State of the American Manager: Analytics and Advice for Leaders.* Gallup: Washington, D.C. www .gallup.com/services/182138/state-american-manager.aspx.

Hedges, K. 2014. "How to Drive Innovation in Five Steps." *Forbes,* April 10. www.forbes.com/sites/work-in-progress/2014/04/10/how-to-drive-innovation-in-five-steps/#10ea70003d4b

Hess, V. 2017. "One Key Healthcare Employee Engagement Strategy That Drives Patient Experience." *Becker's Hospital Review,* May 17. www.beckershospitalreview.com/human-capital-and-risk/one-key-healthcare-employee-engagement-strategy-that-drives-patient-experience.html.

Hogan Assessments. www.hoganassessments.com/products/?category=leadership-development.

Horsager, D. 2009. *The Trust Edge.* New York: Free Press.

HRDQ. 2008. *What's My Communication Style?* West Chester, PA: HRDQ.

Johnston, K. 2012. "Five Steps for Business Problem Solving." *Houston Chronicle,* September 18. http://smallbusiness.chron.com/five-steps-business-problem-solving-55129.html.

Kaiden, S. 2016. *Find Your Fit: A Practical Guide to Landing a Job You'll Love.* Alexandria, VA: ATD Press.

Kantor, J., and D. Streitfeld. 2015. "Inside Amazon: Wrestling Big Ideas in a Bruising Workplace." *New York Times,* August 15. www.nytimes.com/2015/08/16/technology/inside-amazon-wrestling-big-ideas-in-a-bruising-workplace.html.

Kelly, C. 2012. "O.K., Google, Take a Deep Breath." *New York Times,* April 28. www.nytimes.com/2012/04/29/technology/google-course-asks-employees-to-take-a-deep-breath.html.

Knight, R. 2014. "Managing People From 5 Generations." *Harvard Business Review,* September 25. https://hbr.org/2014/09/managing-people-from-5-generations.

Kolko, J. 2012. *Wicked Problems: Problems Worth Solving: A Handbook and a Call to Action.* Austin, Texas: Austin Center for Design.

———. 2015. "Design Thinking Comes of Age." *Harvard Business Review,* September.

Kouzes, J., and B. Posner. *Leadership Practices Inventory (LPI) Assessment.* Hoboken, NJ: John Wiley & Sons.

Kouzes, J.M., and B.Z. Posner. 2012. *The Leadership Challenge: How to Make Extraordinary Things Happen in Organizations.* San Francisco: Jossey-Bass.

Lencioni, P. 2002. *The Five Dysfunctions of a Team: A Leadership Fable.* San Francisco: Jossey-Bass.

———2005. *Overcoming the Five Dysfunctions of a Team: A Field Guide for Leaders, Managers, and Facilitators.* San Francisco: Jossey-Bass.

Locwin, B. 2017. "'Human Error' Deviations: How You Can Stop Creating (Most of) Them." *Pharmaceutical Online,* October 9.

Majcher, K. 2015. "Supermarkets, Startup Style." *MIT Technology Review,* May 26.

Miles-McDonald, D. 2017. "Table of Diversity." Decide Diversity. www.decidediversity.com/table-of-diversity.html.

The Myers & Briggs Foundation. 2018. "MBTI Basics." www.myersbriggs.org/my-mbti-personality-type/mbti-basics.

The Nonprofit Times. 2015. "13 Comparisons of Annual Vs. Major Gifts." *The Nonprofit Times,* November 1. www.thenonprofittimes .com/management-tips/13-comparisons-of-annual-vs-major-gifts.

Oppong, T. 2014. "Don't Just Start a Business, Solve a Problem." *Entrepreneur,* August 15. www.entrepreneur.com/article/236522.

OSHA (Occupational Safety and Health Administration). 2014. *OSHA Pocket Guide. Worker Safety Series: Warehousing.* OSHA. www.osha .gov/Publications/3220_Warehouse.pdf.

Patterson, K., J. Grenny, R. McMillan, and A. Switzler. 2012. *Crucial Conversations: Tools for Talking When Stakes Are High.* New York: McGraw-Hill.

Powell, R. 2015. "Toxic Company Cultures Are Easy in Tech. Here's How the New Wave Is Building Something Better." *The Sydney Morning Herald,* October 9. www.smh.com.au/business/careers/toxic-company -cultures-are-easy-in-tech-heres-how-the-new-wave-is-building-some thing-better-20151008-gk4su0.html.

Press Ganey. 2017. *Performance Insights: Health Care Improvement Trends.* Whitepaper. www.pressganey.com/resources/white-papers /2017-performance-insights-health-care-improvement-trends.

Robinson, D.G., J.C. Robinson, J.J. Phillips, P.P. Phillips, and D. Handshaw. 2015. *Performance Consulting: A Strategic Process to Improve, Measure, and Sustain Organizational Results,* 3rd edition. Oakland, CA: Berrett-Koehler Publishers.

Roush, C. 2013. "Turing a Business Feature Into a Book." *Talking Biz News,* October 22. http://talkingbiznews.com/2/turning-a-business -feature-into-a-book.

Rousmaniere, D. 2015. "What Everyone Should Know About Managing Up." *Harvard Business Review,* January 23. https://hbr.org/2015/01 /what-everyone-should-know-about-managing-up.

Rummler, G.A., and A.P. Brache. 2013. *Improving Performance: How to Manage the White Space on the Organization Chart,* 3rd edition. San Francisco: Jossey-Bass.

Ryan, L. 2017. "The Top Ten Reasons Good Employees Quit." *Forbes,* October 6. www.forbes.com/sites/lizryan/2017/10/06/the-top-ten -reasons-good-employees-quit/#4e8fecd468d0.

Schweitzer, K. 2017. "How to Write and Format a Business Case Study." *ThoughtCo,* September 30. www.thoughtco.com/how-to-write-and -format-a-business-case-study-466324.

Segal, D. 2013. "The Haggler: An Oasis in a Desert of Customer Service." *New York Times,* June 8. www.nytimes.com/2013/06/09/your-money /at-quicken-loans-a-culture-geared-to-customer-service.html.

Shaw, H. 2013. *Sticking Points: How to Get 4 Generations Working Together in the 12 Places They Come Apart.* Carol Stream, IL: Tyndale House Publishers.

Stewart, C. 2014. "How to Identify & Solve Your Business Problems Using Market Research." *Market Research Blog,* June 19. https://blog .marketresearch.com/how-to-identify-solve-your-business-problems -using-market-research.

Sturt, D., and J. Rogers. 2016. "A Global Survey Explains Why Your Employees Don't Innovate." *Harvard Business Review,* February 24. https://hbr.org/2016/02/why-your-employees-dont-innovate.

Target Training International (TTI). n.d. "Who's Who at Your Meeting?" TTI. https://www.ttidisc.com.

Towers Watson. 2014. *2014 Global Workforce Study.* Towers Watson, August 11. www.towerswatson.com/assets/jls/2014_global_workforce _study_at_a_glance_emea.pdf.

Tugend, A. 2015. "Speaking Freely About Politics Can Cost You Your Job." *New York Times,* February 20. www.nytimes.com/2015/02/21 /your-money/speaking-about-politics-can-cost-you-your-job.html.

Watkins, M.D. 2013. *The First 90 Days: Proven Strategies for Getting Up to Speed Faster and Smarter.* Boston: Harvard Business School Publishing.

Willmore, J. 2009. "Getting Past the Five Myths of Employee Motivation and Performance." *ATD Links,* November 4. www.td.org /newsletters/atd-links/getting-past-the-five-myths-of-employee -motivation-and-performance.

———. 2016. *Performance Basics,* 2nd edition. Alexandria, VA: ATD Press.

———. 2017. "Performance Improvement—Where Are We?" (Audio) *TD,* May. www.td.org/magazines/td-magazine/performance -improvementwhere-are-we.

Workplace Fairness. *Today's Workplace: The Workplace Fairness Blog.* www.workplacefairness.org.

ABOUT THE CONTRIBUTORS

Christopher D. Adams

Christopher D. Adams is a performance consultant and instructional designer with more than 20 years of experience helping clients engage people, apply processes, and implement technology to improve human and organizational performance. He is currently a senior consultant for Handshaw Inc. in Charlotte, North Carolina. Chris was co-inventor of Handshaw's award-winning software, Lumenix, one of the first content-managed platforms for e-learning. He has been a featured speaker for a number of ISPI and ATD chapters and has presented at regional and international conferences such as Training Solutions, The Performance Improvement Conference, and the Coast Guard Human Performance Technology Conference. Chris holds degrees in mass communication and instructional systems technology and is currently a doctoral student in the instructional design and technology program at Old Dominion University.

Vivian Blade

Vivian Blade is a recognized talent management expert, guiding companies in designing a leadership talent management framework that builds solid and sustainable bench strength in their leadership pipeline. Additionally, as an author, keynote speaker, trainer, and executive coach, her passion in building leaders and developing excellence empowers organizations and individuals to reach their full potential. In 2009, Vivian founded Experts in Growth Leadership Consulting. She works with many global organizations, such as Johnson & Johnson, Proctor & Gamble, and GE, as well as individual professionals. Vivian is the author of the book *FuelForward: Discover Proven Practices to Fuel Your Career Forward.*

Alan De Back

Alan De Back is an independent career counselor and learning consultant located in the metropolitan Washington, D.C., area. His experience includes more than 20 years in career counseling and learning- and training-related functions. In addition to his current independent role, Alan has served as director of global learning for an Internet consulting firm and manager of leadership development for a major aerospace corporation. His experience also includes roles as a career counselor, trainer, and program manager for a local Northern Virginia government, and assistant director of career services for a major Upstate New York university. Alan holds a bachelor's degree in psychology and history from the State University of New York at Geneseo, a master's degree in human resource development from Rochester Institute of Technology, and a graduate-level certificate in industrial labor relations from Cornell University.

Glen B. Earl

Glen B. Earl is the department chair of the Industrial/Organizational Psychology Program for The Chicago School of Professional Psychology, Dallas, Texas, campus.

Tom Kaiden

Tom Kaiden is the chief operating officer of Visit Alexandria, the conference and visitors bureau for Alexandria, Virginia. He is responsible for strategy, planning, partnerships, finance, and administration. Prior to joining Visit Alexandria, Tom led the Greater Philadelphia Cultural Alliance, the marketing, research, and advocacy association for 300 regional cultural organizations, serving as president (2010–2013) and chief operating officer (2001–2010). Before joining the Cultural Alliance, Tom was the executive director of the Stowe (Vermont) Area Association, where he helped grow four-season revenue at the "Ski Capital of the East" to the point where summer and fall outpaced winter. Previously, he was the director of planning and new business development for S&S

Worldwide, a cataloger serving healthcare and education institutions. Tom began his career in product management with American Express. He holds an MBA from Cornell University and a BA in economics from the University of Connecticut.

Sharlyn Lauby

Sharlyn Lauby is president of ITM Group and author of the blog *HR Bartender*. Prior to starting ITM, Lauby held several senior-level human resources positions in the hospitality, transportation, entertainment, and business services industries. She has designed and implemented successful programs for employee retention, customer satisfaction, and corporate communications. Lauby, a recognized Certified Professional in Learning and Performance (CPLP), is a recipient of the Sam Walton Emerging Entrepreneur award, which recognizes women business owners for their community contributions. She also was named one of the "Heavy Hitters in Human Resources" as compiled by the *South Florida Business Journal*.

Ben Locwin

Ben Locwin has held executive roles for top 10 pharmaceutical companies and has developed human performance models for organizations in startup biotech, hospitals and clinical care centers, aerospace, tech companies, and the energy industry. He is an Advisory Board member for the Association for Talent Development (ATD) and gives speeches to international audiences on improving business performance. Ben has been featured in *Forbes*, the *Wall Street Journal*, the Associated Press, *USA Today*, and other top media.

Rick Rittmaster

Rick Rittmaster, manager of learning and development at MTS, partners with individuals, teams, executives, and external resources to build a more capable and engaged workforce. Working in learning and development, Rick enjoys the sometimes-tricky job of building people-centered solutions that meet MTS's talent management needs. In addition to current learning and development initiatives, Rick also leads initiatives on innovation strategy, performance management, employee engagement, and change management.

Joe Willmore

Joe Willmore is president of the Willmore Consulting Group, a performance consulting firm located near Washington, D.C. He has more than 35 years' consulting experience with a wide range of clients, including the World Bank, Intelsat, Lockheed Martin, the U.S. Navy, Booz Allen Hamilton, and the Smithsonian Institution. He has served on ATD's board of directors and held other leadership positions within ATD and other professional societies.

ABOUT THE AUTHOR

 **Kathryn Stafford** is a publishing industry professional who has been an editor and writer with numerous prestigious institutions, such as the Smithsonian Institution and SI Press. She has written feature stories about problems of conservation and the environment in the Americas, visited newly protected reserves where indigenous communities were transitioning from traditional farming, and interviewed beekeepers, woodworkers, biologists, and union organizers.

An avid long-distance runner and hiker, she competed in the Paris Marathon the last time it was held on a Saturday night and later trekked separatist-filled mountains of Kashmir with her husband, Jeff, and a Buddhist monk companion. When she can, she likes to return to a Maya village in Mexico's Yucatán Peninsula, where she lived for a time between jobs.

Because she's been mired in mud in a Guatemalan jungle, surprised by a coral snake in her toilet in Yucatán, and felled by hypothermia at the end of the Paris marathon, she feels uniquely qualified to write about problems in other murky, meandrous, and chilly places.

Today she lives on seven acres near the western shore of the Chesapeake Bay with Jeff, a beagle, a cat, two chickens, and a vulture family of three.

She is a developmental editor with ATD Press.